An experiment in courage

Mothers of Preschoolers

MOPS International, Inc. // 2370 South Trenton Way // Denver CO 80231-3822 // 303.733.5353 // MOPS.org

Here's to the brave-hearted ones.

The ones who have courage written into their souls,

And the ones who have to find it fresh every day.

To the seekers and some-time finders.

The brilliantly bold mistake-makers.

This is our anthem.

A song that compels us to risk bigger.

With melodies that seep into fear-full places,

Reminding us of who we are.

Whispering the truth that the first step may test our bravery.

But, courage is a key around our necks.

And we were made for this.

May you find the courage to Be you, Bravely.

Heart,

Mandy, Alexandra and Sherry

Table of Contents

Introduction 5

Courage to Raise Brave Kids // Mandy Arioto 6

Courage to Be Extravagant // Mandy Arioto 10

Courage to Forget Comparisons // Sherry Surratt 14

Courage to Be Too Much // Mandy Arioto 17

Courage to Be a Sticky Faith Mom // Mandy Arioto 21

Courage to Forgive and Be Forgiven // Alexandra Kuykendall 27

Courage to Be Honest // Mandy Arioto 30

Courage to Be Generous // Alexandra Kuykendall 34

Courage to Be a Neighbor // Mandy Arioto 37

Courage to Try // Mandy Arioto 40

Courage to Be Intentional // Alexandra Kuykendall 44

Courage to Find Significance in the Everyday // Mandy Arioto 47

The Courage to Face Your Real Mom Fears // Sherry Surratt 50

Courage to Be Broken // Alexandra Kuykendall 53

Courage to Risk // Mandy Arioto 56

Courage to Tell Your Story // Alexandra Kuykendall 59

Courage to Be Passionate // Mandy Arioto 62

Courage to Rest // Alexandra Kuykendall 65

Courage to Be a Mom // Mandy Arioto 68

Courage to Be You, Bravely // Mandy Arioto 72

Authors 78

Introduction

This book is an experiment in courage.

An opportunity to confront the fears that are holding you back.

We decided that the best way to let you know that we are all in this together is to tell you some of our most scary and vulnerable thoughts. That is what you will find in this book. Our real stuff — written out in words and tears and question marks.

You may embark on the journey of going through the book by yourself or with your MOPS group — either way, we are convinced that being brave enough to start is the most thrilling step of all.

At the end of each chapter you will find questions that we are asking ourselves. Feelings that we wrestle with, and think you might too. Use them to help spark thoughts about what courage may look like in your own life. Be open to confronting the hard questions. It may take days or weeks to fully come to terms with your real feelings. Journal, pray, take a walk. Write down your answers. Something important happens when we choose to commit words to paper.

Here is the truth friend: You are a force to be reckoned with. A life-giver and world-changer.

The future beckons to you.

May this experiment with courage remind you of the creative power that breathed life into your bones. May your soul feel like springtime. May you hear the whispers of a dangerous God who calls you to risk bravely and love bigger. And may you find within the pages of this book the courage to Be You, Bravely.

Courage To Raise Brave Kids

by Mandy Arioto

"We all need people in our lives that give us permission to be extraordinary."

— Michael Dauphinee

My brother likes to joke that we were raised by wolves. My parents had a very laid-back parenting style that allowed us to explore, make mistakes, and take risks. In fact, their favorite thing to say to us on a Saturday morning was, "Go outside and have an adventure — and don't come back until you do." This meant that we did a lot of dumb things.

We lived on a farm and had 20 acres of green in which to make mischief. We did dangerous things, swore because no adults were close enough to hear, and learned how to navigate life by working together. I saw a baby horse breathe its first breath in our barn, and held a beloved kitten as he took his last breath. We weren't vaccinated against life — weren't protected from the beauty and pain of each day. Our family invited friends over, my parents drank beer, I took sips and still did fine on my SATs. I saw them struggle financially and relationally, but through it all I felt loved. I knew that I was important and that I had the tools to face tomorrow. I also learned that beauty and pain are soul sisters. Intertwined so tightly that it is difficult to separate one from the other.

Even as an adult, my family is still a little salty. We laugh at jokes that make other people blush. My brother is the life of the party and married to a woman in whom he has met his match. My mom invites new friends — that she just met on the airplane — over for Thanksgiving. And I continue to believe that the rules don't apply to me. We have navigated the premature death of my Dad, in many ways solely because of a very brave mom. To her showing up every day, even when she had nothing to offer, to remind us that we had each other and we were going to make it.

Because of the way I was raised I have never had a particularly hard time with bravery. That is until I held my first baby in my arms and suddenly felt terrified.

I was responsible for another life. And I was fully convinced that it was my hyper vigilance that was going to keep him alive. I was ridiculous — checking on him every hour to make sure he was breathing, and sterilizing his binky any time it came within an inch of floor. Seriously.

But then I pushed another two children out from my body and found myself too tired to employ the same parenting tactics. I was completely worn out. My only goal became making sure everyone was fed by the end of the day. That was it. If we ended the day and everyone was fed, it was a success. Realistic became my new mantra.

We can all agree that there are some universal truths when it comes to this parenting gig. Our job is to keep our children safe, enable them to fulfill their potential, and make sure they're healthy and happy and thriving. I would like to add one more item to that list: I want my kids to feel brave.

I don't know what the deal is with parents in our generation, but so many act as if our kids are porcelain dolls. "Be careful" is on the tip of our tongues, and pumping the brakes is our most comfortable parenting technique.

What I have had to learn from a lot of trial and error is that in order to raise brave kids, I need to be a brave mom. See, scared moms raise scared kids. Brave moms raise brave kids. And modeling bravery doesn't mean we aren't afraid, it just means our actions aren't controlled by our fears. (Jen Hatmaker wrote an amazing blog about this, check out her website at jenhatmaker.com to read " Brave Moms Raise Brave Kids.")

One of my favorite memories of my mom is when I was 8 years old and she rode a horse, even though she was terrified of them. She screamed as she got up into the saddle and was terrified the whole time. But what I remember most is that she did it. And I felt proud to be her daughter.

Here are a few tips that I have learned from the smartest, bravest parents I know:

Have adventures together. Do cool stuff together — especially the stuff that gives wing to the butterflies in your stomach. There is no better way to show kids how to be brave than to do stuff that scares you. Tell them you feel nervous. And then do it anyway.

Talk about everything. Share secrets together. Talk about anything. Ask questions. Share dreams, hopes, concerns. Look them in the eye and listen. If you don't listen to the little things now, they won't share the big things later.

Be OK being wrong. There's an old saying, "The man who knows everything learns nothing." This is particularly true of modeling vulnerability. Let go of the need to always be right. Learn to be okay being wrong and, let your kids be wrong about stuff too. The best way to model bravery is to let our kids know that we all mess up, and it isn't the end of the world.

Struggles make us stronger. When I think about the one thing that makes us deeper people, it would be struggle. Struggle faces failure and forces muscles that are weary with defeat to pick weary bones up off the floor and try again. I have to think that the same thing is true for our kids. Our job as parents isn't to rush to school with their homework so that they don't have to deal with the disappointment of having to stay in at recess. Or to swoop in anytime they are uncomfortable. Our greatest task is to parent them through hard things. Hugging them through moments of failure. Encouraging bravery when they have to confront a friend or apologize for messing up. When we do this our kids will learn how to navigate the real world and will become more compassionate in the process.

Remind them who they are. Tell a kid she is brave and you help her to become so. Speaking bravely over your kids puts words to the picture you have of them and helps them to see themselves the same way.

Become OK with imperfect spirituality. At some point our kids are going to ask hard questions about faith. There is a high likelihood that when they do, they are going to do things that embarrass or disappoint us. They are wrestling with God. Instead of responding with fear, could it be possible that the most redemptive way we engage them is to commend their bravery for asking the hard questions? Could the most courageous thing we do be to trust that God isn't offended, and that in fact it is part of God's redemptive story in their lives?

Trust your kids. Here's the deal, we know kids are drawn to the things that make our parental palms sweat: high places, water, wandering far away, dangerous sharp tools. Our instinct is to keep them safe by childproofing their lives. The truth is, a relaxed approach to risk taking actually keeps our kids safer by honing their judgment of what they're capable.

So friends, may you have the courage to push the accelerator.
May you scream as you hop into the saddle and bask in the glory of proud kids.
And may you leave a legacy of brave for generations to come.

Now, go outside and have an adventure. And don't come back until you do.

Questions

How did my childhood shape my courage as an adult?

What are my biggest fears about letting my kids take risks?

What do I do that is brave that is modeling courage to my kids?

What is one thing I can do this week to raise brave kids?

Courage To Be Extravagant

by Mandy Arioto

"Aim to be stunningly inefficient with your love." — Bob Goff

Sometimes I can feel the house breathing. Its breath smells like a mixture of stained wood, musty basement and fabric softener. It is a smell that stays with you, that is seared in your memory for a lifetime.

We moved almost every other year when I was young, so I never really had the opportunity to become attached to the houses we lived in or the neighbors next door. But there was one place that was my home base. A tiny brown house on Alpha Street. A house that breathed love into my soul.

The carpet on the stairs was burnt orange, and I spent many afternoons sitting on a landing half way up and looking at the swirling pattern of the carpet while adults talked and ate. I never really heard what was being said but that was OK, because I felt what was happening. I think that is the beauty of being a child. The words matter, but not nearly as much as the feeling does.

You know when you are getting close to the tiny brown house, because you drive past the greasy burger joint called the Char-pit and then up Lake Avenue. When you see the corner store you know you are almost to Alpha Street.

For me, Alpha Street meant home, and home smelled like love.

In the summertime, my brother and I would stay with Grandma Joan who lived in the little brown house for weeks at a time. We had lemonade stands in the front yard and walked to Lake Ontario. Our favorite thing to do was to run as fast as we could, jump, and then cannonball into the waves. We had contests to see who could make the biggest splash. Grandma would sit on the edge of the water, making designs in the sand with a feather and cheering us on. Time was measured in love, and we had eons of it.

Whenever we arrived at Grandma Joan's brown house, she would be sitting out on the stairs by the front door, waiting for the moment we arrived. We would explode from the car and she would meet us halfway down the walk, wrapping us in bear hugs. It was as if she was seeing us for the first time, savoring the sight of us. She hugged us so much that we nearly melted. It was quite a scene. Mrs. Beauchamp who lived across the street would peer out her window, wondering what all of the commotion was about.

After all the hugging, we would go inside and I would sit on the plaid couch propped up by pillows and home-stitched blankets. I would sip tea with too much sugar, and pick cookies out of the Winnie-the-Pooh cookie jar. We talked and colored. She let me try on all of her jewelry. The best part was just being with my grandma, sharing breath and tea and hugs.

At night, she'd tuck us into bed in the blue room. That is what we called it. It was a cozy room with navy blue paint on the walls and a window seat that looked out over the street. Grandma Joan would kiss our cheeks and then tell us stories about the great Garloo who lived down the bathtub drain. She made up stories that left us believing that anything was possible. We would beg her to tell us more, and she would oblige until our eyelids grew heavy. And then she would tiptoe out of the room, leaving the door open just a crack so that the light shone through enough that we would never feel scared.

Love filled every nook and cranny of the brown house. Grandma Joan made us feel like the whole world was beautiful and filled with potential. Extravagant love has a way of making wonder possible.

Years later, Grandma Joan and I sit on her couch in the tiny brown house. We both know it is our last visit. We sit and watch her first great-grandson, my first baby, play with her jewelry on the carpet. I fumble words trying to speak back to her all of the love that she has given to me. Nothing feels adequate.

Then she fills in the gaps, "My beauty, I love you infinitely, but it is Jesus who makes all of this real."

And I know in my bones what she means. Without the love of a God who pursues and gives without restraint, we wouldn't have this extravagant love that waits for us on the stairs, and splashes in the waves and kisses our cheeks.

It was the best church I have ever experienced.

Two years ago, I decided that I wasn't living up to my legacy. I needed more love in my life. And realizing that I can't force people to love me better, I decided to start loving them better. Feeling love extravagantly wasn't going to be enough for me anymore. I needed to express it. So, my mantra became to think less and love more. I stopped worrying about how my every action was going to be perceived, and I gave myself permission to be extravagant. Loving big takes courage.

Extravagant love does heists of generosity toward our enemies. It refuses to believe that there isn't hope. It shows up at my friend's house, whose life is in ruins because she cheated on her husband so that I can clean her dishes and remind her that Jesus isn't afraid of messes. It refuses to let the fact that my Dad couldn't tell me that he loved me keep me from telling the people I love, just how crazy I am about them. It saves us from ourselves. It moves us intentionally toward relationships instead of finding differences. And when we love like this, people might not know what to do with us. They might look at us like there's something wrong with us. But there isn't. It's what we were born to do.

Extravagant love looks different because it is unreasonable and everyone is included. Many people of faith seem to believe that God needs to be protected, and so we decide who is in and who is out. Who is loved and who isn't. This shows up for me when I am tired and stressed. I know this because it starts to feel like I don't have enough to give. Like I have to scrimp and save to make sure I don't run out. When I feel like I don't have anything left to give, my love isn't as gloriously messy or spontaneous anymore — I get stingy and polite. But polite is just about the worst way to love someone that I can imagine.

Loving extravagantly requires a willingness to walk to the lake.

So, cannonball life. Get a running start, make the biggest splash possible and get everyone around you soaking wet. Make a huge scene. You and I weren't meant to be afraid of stuff — but to go for it with every fiber of our being. Love in ways that sweep other people off their feet — so that no one has any question whether the extravagant love — the love that saves you — is the real deal.

Because, my beauty, Jesus makes all of this real.

Questions

Have I ever been loved extravagantly before? What was it like?

What is holding me back from extravagantly loving others?

What adjective would I use to describe the current state of how I love others? Messy? Polite?

What is one thing I can do this week to love extravagantly?

Courage To Forget Comparisons

by Sherry Surratt

"Sometimes what you fear the most is the very thing that will set you free." — Robert Tew

When she opened her refrigerator door, I thought, You have got to be kidding! The shelves were pristine, with the milk lined neatly against one side, flanked by the bottles of orange and cranberry juice, all on the shelf labeled drinks. Everything had its place, in an order that made sense, with the cheeses and lunch meats in their special drawer and the items in the crisper actually looking fresh and crisp. The wild thought flicked across my brain to salute the contents of her refrigerator to see if they would snap to attention and salute back. I sighed as I thought of my fridge at home. An empty milk jug on the middle shelf (could someone please throw it away when you've drained the last drop?), leftovers with good intentions that long ago had lost any resemblance to the food they once were. If I had to fix a decent meal for surprise guests who dropped in, I would be hard pressed with the lack of decent ingredients. And I certainly wouldn't want to open the fridge, lest they see the chaos within.

Joan's refrigerator made me think "organized" and "well stocked." Mine? It made me feel depressed.

But this was how I often felt when I went to Joan's house. She was so well-thought-out and put together. She exercised every morning, planned her meals a week in advance, and never seemed flustered or rushed. Her house was beautiful and her closet organized by color. She could find anything in her purse at a moment's notice (I could build a summer house out of dryer lint in the time I've wasted digging in my purse.) After spending time with Joan I often I wished I could be like her.

What is it about someone else's strengths that makes us notice our weaknesses? I can sing. I can teach a children's class and plan and lead an event. But keep my refrigerator clean and my pantry organized? Behind closed (refrigerator) doors, I was a sorry mess.

This is the danger of comparisons. It makes you forget the wonderful about you, and focus on the not-so-good. And when we compare ourselves with someone who excels at what we don't, our weaknesses grow even bigger in our own eyes. Every woman has beauty and talent of her own, so why do we crave the beauty and talent we see in someone else? I think sometimes when we like what we see in someone else, all of a sudden the positive trait we notice becomes monumental. She's all of that, and I'm none of that and I never will be.

God tells me in his Word that I am beautifully and wonderfully made (Psalm 139). It's sometimes hard to believe this when I step out of the shower, dripping wet, and catch a full glimpse of me in my unvarnished and unadorned glory. Does God not know the definition of beautiful? He must be mistaken because there are days when I'm sure I'm anything but. But I'm learning this is Satan's plan, which is totally opposite of what God wants for me. Throughout God's Word he tells me what he sees when he looks at me: a mom full of promise and a heart filled with love, a wife that wants to delight her husband, a woman who has gifts and talents that are unlike anyone else, that she can use to make a difference.

I can know this in my head, but it's another thing to really live it.

Here's how I daily try to let this sink into my life:

The art of thankfulness. I've come to realize that gratitude really is an art form — something to study and learn. As I practice how to really be thankful, I realize it takes my comparing eyes off of others, and forces me to delight in what God has given me to enjoy. It brings forward a feeling of being blessed, which shuts down my desire to pick at myself. When I take time to really be thankful for the life I choose to lead, with the children and husband I live it with, it eats up the space I would normally fill with noticing what I don't have or what I'm not.

Build off of your strengths. It has taken me a while to realize what I'm really good at, and to appreciate the value of my talents. How about you? Do you know what your strengths are? Start with identifying what you love doing. Chances are, you are really good at it. Then look for opportunities to use this gift to bless somebody else. Are you a great cook? Look for opportunities where bringing a meal could really make someone feel loved or could lighten their day. Are you an encourager? A well-chosen word can literally change the way someone feels about herself and turn their day around. Take a new look at what you are gifted at, no matter how small you might think it is, and pour yourself into it.

The power of self-talk. Would you talk to others the way you talk to yourself? Pay attention to that voice in your head and if it's not a nice one, redirect it. Remind yourself of the good stuff, the parts of you that are wonderful (there are lots of them) and stop yourself when your thoughts start to compare you with someone else. I rely on great go-to verses that remind me of what God says about me, like Zephaniah 3:17, "The Lord is with you wherever you go. He is mighty to save you. He will take great delight in you and quiet you with his love. He rejoices over you with singing." God knows you better than anyone else, and if he declares you delightful just the way you are, then you truly are!

Are you ready to let go of the comparisons?

Questions

What don't I like about myself, and from where did this originate?

What are the lies that I have bought into about myself?

What are three positive statements about myself as a woman, wife or mom that I know to be true?

What is one way that I can use my strengths to help another mom?

How can I lean into what God says about me? Do I have a go-to verse that helps me in times of self-doubt?

Courage To Be Too Much

by Mandy Arioto

"Nothing is more powerful than allowing yourself to truly be affected by things. Whether it's a song, a stranger, a mountain, a rain drop, a tea kettle, an article, a sentence, a footstep ... feel it all ... Take it and have gratitude." — Zooey Deschanel

It is late at night. Everyone in my little house is sleeping and I am sitting here thinking I should tell you my secrets. In what is sure to be the equivalent of a late night text to an ex-boyfriend I am going to reveal something I may regret in the light of day.

The truth is that sometimes I hide.

See, I have a tendency to keep some feelings hidden, afraid to go too far. Ever since I was little I have felt the need to play small because if I don't — if I show the fullness of who I am, then everyone will think that I am too much.

I cry at songs and can literally feel other people's emotions. I love to celebrate big and show other people how much I love them. But often I feel like I shouldn't share my emotions because they are so big.

I almost lost it at Charlotte's soccer game on Saturday. A dad from the other team who happened to be sitting within hearing range of us kept making comments about how he wanted to "beat the sh*t out of number 10" on our team because he felt like she was pushing a player on his team. What? These children are 5 years old. And did I mention that number 10 is MY child? At the end of the game as the players high fived one another and gathered on the sideline to distribute snacks, I walked to the porta-potty on the side of the field and ugly cried. I needed to regain my composure and crying it out seemed like the only available technique. I wanted to tear the dad's head off and use some of my own choice words to convey to this adult parent what I thought of him. Like I said ... BIG emotions.

I've spent a whole lot of my life trying to be different than I really am. Trying to be less of everything. Less sensitive. Less sentimental. Less me. Trying to make it appear like I have everything in balance. Dulling my creativity to stay in the lines. I just want to be acceptable. Presentable. I want to fit in.

I am pretty sure it started in high school. (Can I get an amen, friends?)

My family had just moved to a new town and I wanted to fit in. But the first acquaintance I met said things to me like, "You dress weird, you think too much, you laugh too loudly."My soul felt sunburned. Like I had been overexposed, and all I wanted was to be healed from all this feeling and being.

I didn't want to stand out or have my differences noticed. So I talked myself into believing that I had to make myself smaller. And I shrank, suffering from a year-long battle with an eating disorder as a result of needing to literally make myself less. I was afraid to fill my space in this world.

But I am not OK with that kind of thinking anymore.

I don't know whether it is the accumulation of years or hearing family friends share about my dad at his funeral that is saving me in this department. Dad was a passionate person. He coached football and would get so worked up on the sidelines that his face would become red and he would yell or cheer at the top of his lungs. You couldn't ignore him. And at his funeral, one person after another got up to share about how he influenced them, about how they appreciated his passion and how it was his 'too much' that they loved most about him.

What I learned is that perfection is boring. It is uniqueness that is compelling. We fall in love with each other's rough edges. Our "too much" makes us endearing.

For me, giving myself permission to be too much means that I show up in big ways. I bring a gift when it isn't expected, I re-write a song for a friend's fortieth birthday and force my husband to perform it with me. I go out of my way to let people know how much I love them. I give myself permission to feel. This can be embarrassing for my kids. They question why I need to dance in a store when my favorite song comes on. My husband wonders why I have to put so much extra effort into picking out the perfect gift and maybe gets a little frustrated when I insist on including him in my shenanigans. Without fail though, we will be driving home and he will acknowledge that things are better when I go big.

Giving ourselves permission to be too much doesn't mean that we can spew our emotions all over everyone else. It doesn't mean that we can bulldoze other people or make them responsible for how we are feeling. What it does mean is that we are free from overanalyzing our every move. We get to live in the freedom that our uniqueness is a gift to the world. Meant to be shared. Meant to be lived.

The world doesn't need more people hiding the truth of who we really are beneath uniforms of conformity. What it needs are more people who are brave enough to come out of hiding. We need more insanely brave people who are willing to offer their too much to the world.

What if we stop trying to fit into other people's expectations?

What if we stop worrying about what other people are going to think?

What if we wore the outfit that makes us happy instead of the cultural uniform that magazines tell us is fashionable?

What if we gave ourselves permission to celebrate big and cry at songs that move us?

What if we gave ourselves the freedom to stand out?

Instead of striving for balance, may you strive for that which moves you.

May you resist the urge to shrink.

May you experience the freedom of living fully and encourage others to do the same.

May you be *too much*.

Questions

Can I remember a time when I felt like I wanted to shrink? What was the experience?

Can I remember a time when I was fully myself? What was the experience?

What are the ways I sometimes feel like "too much"?

Thinking about my best friend, what do I love about her that she might feel like is too much?

What is one thing I can do this week to embrace my too much?

Courage To Be a Sticky Faith Mom

by Mandy Arioto

"Children live in a world of dreams and imagination, a world of aliveness ... There is a voice of wonder and amazement inside all of us; but we grow to realize we can no longer hear it, and we live in silence. It isn't that God stopped speaking; it is that our lives became louder."

— Mike Yaconelli

We live in Denver.

In the winter my kids refuse to wear jackets. My son will even go to school in shorts because junior highers are cool like that. For a long time I fought it. Practically holding him down and forcing him to put on gloves and ear muffs and a jacket. I was worried about how other moms would judge me when my kid showed in a snowstorm in shorts.

And then I decided that it was his deal. His decision if he was going to be cold. His decision about how he wanted to feel on the way to school. And so I gave up, packed away the ear muffs and scarves and filled his drawer with shorts.

I embraced it.

I know now, that it is very unlikely you will ever invite me to speak at a parenting conference. This will be even more true when I tell you more of our reality.

We go to church with homeless people downtown and invite kids over who use bad words. We send our kids to public school and I often have to break up fights between two brothers who meet us at our bus stop and whose favorite word to yell at each other is, "A**hole." I let my kids use knives to cut veggies, and I had no sleep rules when we raised our babies. Most nights we end up with four people and a dog in our bed because two of our three kids have snuck in in the middle of the night. We take our kids on scary hikes and encourage them to rock climb sheer cliffs because they can.

And now, after all that, I am about to say something that may make you really uncomfortable.

I have a problem with church.

Especially the way we teach kids at church.

It seems to me that so much of how the church messages kids about a faith experience is focused on raising gentlemen and ladies who are civilized, collected, rule followers.

We do the same thing with God — we try to round off the edges. To make God more palatable, pretty, civilized. I have friends who fiercely guard how much of the Bible that they share with their kids because they are worried that some of the stories are too violent or scary.

Have you read the stories that God has offered us as his words to the world? They are messy and violent and will make you blush. It is exactly the kind of content that I try to shield my kids from more of the time. But can I tell you that those parts are my kids' favorite? They love the breathtaking unpredictability of a God who invites people who have messed up big — bigger than people in our modern day prison system — and then takes their lives and uses them to slay giants and change the world.

The thing that I love most about Jesus is that he had no patience for religious types who were drowning in their own self righteousness. He preferred to spend his time with the ragamuffins, the ones on the periphery who did things that made other people uncomfortable.

And it seems to me that if Jesus came to my house today he would show up as the bachelor uncle. The one who arrives with extravagant gifts and feeds the kids chocolate before bed, despite my disapproving tendency to want everything to run according to my predetermined schedule. He would look them in the eye and throw his head back in laughter about the joke they just made up, and then give them bear hugs that squeeze all of the air out of their lungs. He would tell them scary stories about the adventures he has had, and the bad guys he has confronted. My kids would fight to sit next to him, not wanting to leave his side because they might miss something. Jesus would play in the back yard and encourage the kids to jump off a tree stump from a height that feels just scary enough. He would challenge them to risk more than is comfortable and to love as big as they can. They would learn to stand up to bullies and share their snacks with the kids who don't have enough.

But sadly, this isn't the Jesus most of us meet along the way. More often, the faith that we pick up is full of rules and regulations. I can't tell you how many friends have shared stories with me about growing up afraid of messing up and disappointing God rather than being wooed by an extravagant God. I have seen too many kids who are raised in a Christian home end up completely indifferent to faith. Some of them feel betrayed by hypocrisy that they have witnessed in the church but more often it is the result of nothing more than boredom. We wonder why they run as fast as they can to find an adventure. We have failed to show them that following Jesus is the greatest adventure on which they could embark.

I want my kids to do what is right out of love instead of fear. Religion is held together by rules and rituals. Following Jesus is fueled by passion and mission. As Erwin McManus says in his book, *Soul Cravings* (Thomas Nelson, 2008), "If our children are going to walk away from Jesus, I want to raise them in a way that they understand that to walk away from Jesus is to walk away from a life of faith, adventure and risk, and to choose a life that, without Him, is boring, mundane and ordinary."

My 12 year old had the opportunity to accompany my husband on a business trip to Israel this year. It was a two-week adventure filled with all sorts of unique experiences like riding bikes through the ancient city to visit bakeries making Challah bread for Sabbath, praying at the Wailing Wall, and picking up a stone from the Elah valley where a young David defeated Goliath. For weeks after he got home we would find him sneaking to stay up late to read the Bible. Instead of turning off his light at nine, which is bedtime, he would close his door to hide the light so that he could read about the stories he heard about on his trip. Joe and I hadn't done anything to encourage him to read, he was simply captivated by the stories of God. He had experienced it firsthand and was so consumed that he had to know more.

I am a firm believer that what we do as parents says more about what we believe than what we keep telling our kids about what we believe. Because of that, we don't do family Bible studies because I would rather have my kids see us doing things rather than talking about them. Instead, we read the words God wrote down and then when we find something that sparks a question or compels us to act, we do it. We pick up and move, we give more than makes sense, we make cupcakes for our neighbor. Whoever in our family hears God whispering in their hearts, we talk about it and do something about it.

I want my kids to be compelled to follow the crazy voice of Jesus rather than the conforming voice of religion. The most compelling times I have heard Jesus are the times when I needed to act big and do something that didn't make sense. I can only gather that it will be the same thing in my kids' lives. And I don't, after all, want them to be wearing ear muffs because I am too worried about what other people will think.

I want them to be more worried about what God is for, than what he is against.

I want my kids to have the ability to see the invisible and hear the inaudible because their hearts know God.

I desperately want this kind of faith and relationship with God for each of my three kids, but here is the truth, I know that I am not enough to make that happen. It is going to take a community surrounding each of my kids in every stage of their growing-up years to cheer them on toward adventurous faith.

You need to meet my mom. My kids call her Nene and she is one of the most lovely and real people you will ever meet. There are so many things I appreciate about the way she raised us, but one of my favorites is a tradition she started on our birthdays. Each year my mom writes a blessing for every member of our family on our birthday. It feels matriarchal and deep and biblical. We tease her sometimes because of how seriously she takes it but we secretly love it. She signs each one with a photo of herself doing a handstand, reminding us that we shouldn't take ourselves too seriously. I have been compiling every blessing that she has given to my kids and I've put them in a book, one for each kid. My hope is that when I hand them their blessings when they turn 18, it will be heavy with tradition. That they'd know that the prayers of generations surround them, intercede for them, and have gone before them every step of the way. That the prayers and blessings of Nene took on flesh and blood, were put into action, and transformed into wonderful memories. And that they will treasure their faith and the people who formed it as each of them sets out on their own one day.

Kara Powell is a professor at Fuller Theological Seminary who has written numerous books and done countless hours of research on what kids need to develop a faith that lasts. In her book, *Sticky Faith* (Zondervan, 2011), she shares the results of her research with parents. Here are four essential things she says we can do for our kids in order to actively participate in their faith journey in ways that will have long-lasting implications:

Connect your kids to at least five caring adults. Kids need to develop a strong personal identity for faith to stick, and community helps do just that. When kids know specific adults who are "on their team," they have a web of support to catch them when they fall and keep them connected to faith for the long haul. Using the scaffolding of existing relationships with extended family, neighbors, friends, coaches and teachers, build a 5:1 (or 7:1, or 10:1, or whatever you determine works best for your family) sticky web adult to child ratio for mentoring your kids. Other adults are often able to speak to them in ways you cannot as the parent.

Ask your kids who they will turn to when they have doubts. Doubt in and of itself isn't toxic; it's unexpressed doubt that turns toxic. One of the repeated themes in the research was the importance of parents giving their kids space to wrestle with tough faith questions until they pinned down their own answers. Giving permission for independent thought leads to lasting faith.

Share verbally about your own faith journeys. Stop lecturing your kids or interviewing them; instead, share organically about your own faith. Use time in the car, recent current events, or dinner discussions as a chance to share how your own faith is growing, or ways that your faith impacts your everyday life. Include both a sense of your present religious experiences and insights as well as highlights of your faith journey in the past.

Reinforce that their faith is bigger than any moral failure or mistake. As children and teens navigate faith through developmental markers, they may see faith as a list of behaviors, akin to what Dallas Willard calls the "gospel of sin management." Tragically, when students with that view of their faith fail, their feelings of guilt cause them to run from their faith and the church, just when they need them the most. A faith that sticks is one that is based not primarily on behaviors, but on a life affirming truth that we are the most whole when we are part of a relationship with God.

Questions

What was your faith experience as a kid? How did you view God? How did that play into how your faith journey has evolved as an adult?

How do you want your kids to experience faith?

How does this view of a faith journey make you feel?

What is one thing you can do this week to inspire your kids toward faith?

Courage To Forgive and Be Forgiven

by Alexandra Kuykendall

"The man who makes no mistakes does not usually make anything." — Edward John Phelps

To say I raised my voice would be putting it mildly — and I don't yell at my husband. After reading this, of course, you'll know that's not true… I should say I rarely yell at my husband. But the perfect storm of PMS, stress, exhaustion, recent work disappointments and of course our ever present four children, led me to lash out in a way that got me some attention.

"You think this sounds selfish. Don't you?" I asked. I wanted him to say it. That the one thing I was requesting from our family schedule was selfish.

"Well, it is all about you." That was all I needed.

"NOTHING. I HAVE NOTHING THAT'S ALL ABOUT ME. THIS. IS. IT."

The look on Derek's face showed I'd probably crossed the line in my passion level when conveying this message. And what could possibly have been causing this level of frustration and anger you might ask? We were late leaving for church that morning. Ummm… overreacting? Well, it's complicated. As most fights in marriage are, right?

For a year I'd been asking my husband to pull out of our driveway at 10:15 on Sunday mornings. I'd give him the one hour, half hour and ten minute countdowns until departure time. It's the one consistent point in the week when all six of us have to be dressed, fed and out the door at the same time, and I told him I resented having to get five people ready to leave while he only had to get one. And in my frustrated mind, we were late every time.

But of course that all depends on how you define the word late. Walking into the sanctuary while the first song is playing (and the majority of our congregation is also arriving) is not late in Derek's book. But for me, I like to arrive and be settled in my spot ready to enjoy a total of three songs (that's it — three songs) for my weekly communal worship time. Because here's the thing — our church serves snacks. It's a wonderful addition for a family to have goldfish crackers and grapes provided at the back of the sanctuary, but it also means as soon as we get there, four girls are asking me to go back with them and hold their cups of water while they scoop mini-pretzels from a bowl onto their paper plates. With the two-year old always spilling hers, of course. And then kids are dismissed to Sunday School, and at least one always wants Mommy to be the escort. And those three longed-for songs disappear into one and a half on a good day. And that morning I ended up standing with my mouth moving to words of worship while I was fuming at my husband for being late again. Because I Just. Wanted. Three. Songs.

I had convinced myself that this apparently casual overlook on his part was actually a respect issue. There was a progression of offense growing in my head and it came out in me being hysterical about getting to church on time. And my husband laughing at how ironic it was that I was irate over such a holy matter didn't help. It's all just silly I know, but in the moment I was mad and hurt because it felt symbolic of our family's priorities, and that my desires were at the bottom of them.

Had he broken some enormous trust? No. Committed some life-altering offense? No. But in my mind that little seed of anger was watered, sprouted, grew and blossomed into a monumental infraction. This is how most of the conflict in our marriage works. One of us takes something small and instead of addressing it head on, stews and grows the incident out of proportion. And in this case I had the morning, my time at church, and lunch at home to let it all swell before I exploded.

And after said explosion and lots of crying on my part (which confirmed to me that indeed PMS was involved) we reconciled.

"I'm sorry. I see now it represented more to you," he said.

"I'm sorry. I overreacted. I just have so few windows in my week where I'm not taking care of somebody else," I said. (Have you felt like that, too?)

It was a coming back together. An "I love you more than I love being right" kind of moment. But the courage to say I forgive you was a surrender on my part to being right on this issue. All of my assertions were true. We did pull out of the driveway late, I did get everyone dressed, I did give the departure countdown every week. But I was able to forgive those things because we are two imperfect people trying to make a relationship work, and I can't hold on to the small things.

And asking for forgiveness took courage because I had to look at myself a little more honestly. Despite the fact that my assertions were correct, I was fallible all over the place. What I offer our marriage is a broken woman who loses it more than she should. And I so appreciate that Derek hasn't given up on me, just as I haven't given up on him. And I needed to look at the underlying issue: I was afraid to say I needed something. I needed time to myself. I was afraid that was selfish, and that he would see it as such. I had to humbly face all of those things, and that took courage.

In this case I was reconciling with someone I trust. Sometimes we are called to forgive people who have hurt us in some way, and it isn't smart or safe to stay in a relationship with them. But because God forgave us we must still offer that olive branch of forgiveness, so the bitterness doesn't eat us up inside. Either way, when we mend a relationship or let go of a hurt, forgiveness provides our soul with some reconciliation with people, and God allows us to move forward instead of staying stuck.

There is no question the larger the hurt, the more difficult it may be to forgive. This minor disagreement was just that. It wasn't threatening the future of our marriage. But in addressing these little needs for forgiveness as soon as they arise, our relationship stays healthy. This acts as a safeguard against larger trust issues seeping in. And every time I've yielded to releasing through forgiveness, no matter how small the incident, the healing has come more quickly. Not always instantly, but at least more quickly. For the sake of my family — and my own sanity — I want to be a woman who doesn't hold on to bitterness, but who forgives frequently and with a genuine heart.

Questions

How do conflicts sprout in my house?

Are there moments when it's easier for me to forgive than others? Why or why not?

Is it easier for me to forgive, or to be forgiven?

Is there someone I need to forgive? If so, what is keeping me from forgiving?

Is there someone I need to ask for forgiveness?

How are trust and forgiveness intertwined in my life?

How can I foster a culture of forgiveness in my home?

Courage To Be Honest

by Mandy Arioto

"The greatest gift you ever give is your honest self." — Fred Rogers

I am going to tell you a story that I was told not to share with you. My brother says it is going to make you think horrible thoughts about me. But I am all about full disclosure. So here it is — the dirty truth... During college I dated four different guys at the same time. And they didn't know about each other. I was the bad guy (girl...) in a not-so-romantic comedy, and there isn't a happy ending to this story.

[If you want to hear the whole unedited story you can watch me tell it here www.mandyarioto.com]

The short version is that I had just broken up with a long-term boyfriend and for whatever reason, four different guys asked me out on dates within a few weeks of each other. Because they were each so different — and let's be honest here — totally good looking, I decided to go on dates with each one. It all started out very innocently, but as the weeks went by, I found myself falling for each guy for different reasons. I was getting scared that they were going to find out about one another. My roommates were having to cover for me, I couldn't answer my phone, and I was sneaking around to avoid getting caught. I had created a tangled mess.

How untrue I was being to each of these guys — of course the story ends horribly. I was out with one guy when I ran into another one of the guys. (Sidebar: It really is a great story. You should watch me tell it onscreen so you can frown in disapproval and make tsk tsk sounds as I tell it.) There was a messy confrontation and instead of having four great guys to date, I ended up with zero.

At the end of the whole ordeal my heart was broken and my head was just barely inhabitable. I thought such awful thoughts about myself that I cannot even say them out loud because they would make Jesus want to binge eat a whole bag of Hershey's kisses. I was humiliated and embarrassed that I hadn't been honest sooner — like from the beginning. Have you ever done something that put you in a situation where you dreaded being found out? Or a time when you were scared to be honest?

I know what it feels like to carry things with you. You need to confess, but the words feel too heavy to speak out loud. And then when you muster a moment of courage that allows you to speak your secrets into existence, they suddenly seem so much less powerful. To me, honesty feels like I have been holding my breath for a long time and finally get to exhale. The longer I hold it in, the more desperate I am to breathe.

Hard conversations are my kryptonite. They make me sweaty and uncomfortable. I have relied too heavily on niceness for most of my life, which means that I have had the tendency to round off the edges. When I say hard things in the nicest, non-emotion-evoking way possible, the words often end up meaning nothing at all.

My need to have everyone love me once convinced me that I couldn't be honest. But that didn't serve anyone well. The people who I loved most — my friends and family — never got my whole self. They got Nice Mandy, but they often missed out on Honest Mandy. I value honesty so much from everyone around me, desperately wanting to know their honest truths, but I was never willing to offer myself to others in that way. And so, I am working on being more direct and confrontational when appropriate.

Becoming a mom has helped me tremendously. It gave me the courage to use my voice. Suddenly I was free to express my needs in a new way because I was advocating for the needs of my babies. I wasn't afraid to ask for what they needed from doctors, from teachers or from strangers at the playground. I suddenly knew what I wanted and was able to ask for it because I was advocating for them. No conversation was too scary when it was for the good of my babies. And now I realize that I have that same freedom in advocating for myself by asking for what I need, saying no or having hard conversations.

My husband Joe and I work hard to make truth-telling easy in our family, because honesty is a high priority to us. I don't want my kids to carry around anything that they don't have to. I would rather hear the truth about what they are feeling or doing than have them think that there are secrets that need to be hidden because they are too dirty or shameful to be shared. I am a firm believer that secrets make us sick.

At our house, every topic is open for discussion. My kids ask questions about sex, injustice and are keenly interested in discussing cuss words and why we shouldn't use them. Yesterday in the car my daughter shared with me about the two times that she lied at school in kindergarten two years ago. I think she needed to get it off of her chest.

Here's the hard part. Truth-telling is embarrassing. It exposes our guts to the world and to our friends and to our spouses. Early in our relationship I was embarrassed to tell Joe what I needed because I didn't want to be perceived as needy or demanding. But he missed out on being my partner in the ways that fulfilled me most, because he wasn't aware of what I needed.

Hiding from the truth causes us to feel alone and can turn the thin cracks in our lives into deep gaping chasms. Often when this happens, we end up filling in the gaps with things that don't serve us well. There was a point in my life where I filled in my gaps with exercise. Other times it was with sleep or over-commitment. Busy-ness is another way I keep myself from confronting the real issues that need my attention.

For so long I felt like I had to manage my external relationships. I would coach Joe on how he talked about his job, worried that he would be perceived a certain way. I worried about what people would think or how they would judge the unconventional decisions we make. I was my own full time PR person — and it was exhausting.

Whether we are managing other people's perceptions of us or hiding things because of shame, our secrets hold us captive.

So in an effort to live unencumbered, every once in a while I will ask myself, "Do I have anything going on in my life that no one knows about?" And if I do, then it might be time to get honest with someone. Because the only thing worse than struggling, is struggling in secrecy.

I believe in truth telling because honesty is medicinal. It has healing qualities that neutralizes the fears that make us sick. When we speak secrets out loud it breaks their power over us.

In the last month, I've had to get honest with my closest friends. We are talking ugly honest. Where they see my most unsavory truths and continue to show up in spite of it. And I was reminded is that friends help everything.

So often we think we are the only one. The only one who thinks judging thoughts about the too-pretty-to-be-friends-with mom at the bus stop. The only one whose marriage feels fragile. The only one who shames herself because she would rather hide in the bathroom than pretend to lose at Candyland for the sixty-eighth time.

When we share our most vulnerable truths, asking friends to pray for us or to offer insight, we become free. Our shame no longer holds us prisoner. We allow other people to whisper "me too," and realize we are not alone anymore. And in sharing our own struggles we free our friends to be able to share theirs.

"Writer Anne Lamott says that the most powerful sermon in the world is two words, 'Me too.'Me too. When you're struggling, when you are hurting, wounded, limping, doubting, questioning, barely hanging on, moments away from another relapse, and somebody can identify with you — someone knows the temptations that are at your door, somebody has felt the pain that you are feeling, when someone can look you in the eyes and say, 'Me too,' and they actually mean it — it can save you."

*Rob Bell, *Jesus Wants to Save Christians: Learning to read a dangerous book* (HarperOne, 2012), pg 151.

Here is the truth: anytime I have been brave enough to lay it all out before my friends, confessing my biggest struggles, trusting them with my stuff, I have walked away a better person. No. Joke.

My friends remind me that I am brave and kind and not defined by my failures.

It is in the eyes of people who love us that we come to know ourselves. So, let's create safe spaces where we can be truth-tellers. Places where whole is more valuable than pretty. Where honest is prized more than comfortable. And let's be families where we don't have to posture or hide, but where we allow one another to spill our guts so that we are free to live whole and loved.

Questions

Do I have anything going on in my life that no one else knows about?

Are there any conversations I have been avoiding or putting off because they feel too hard?

Which areas in my life are the hardest to be honest about?

What is one thing I can do this week to be more honest?

Courage To Be Generous

by Alexandra Kuykendall

"Never suppress a generous thought." — Camilla E. Kimball

I wrote the names of friends from church with the corresponding children's names on the spreadsheet atop my clipboard as people took the ornaments from the Christmas tree in our church lobby. I felt like I knew each child whose ornament was being selected. I'd read notes and gift requests from their parents in prison, talked to their caregivers on the phone to get permission for them to receive a Christmas gift from their incarcerated parent, and written down the toy each child hoped for and most recent clothing sizes. I'd prayed for each family separated this Christmas season, and recruited my husband and kids to deliver the gifts Christmas Eve day. I waited until the post-worship dwellers were done clearing out of the lobby before I took the last four ornaments off the tree for our family, and added our names to the spreadsheet. I was one prepared and organized giver.

December is a terrible time to be generous from a logistical standpoint. Like many COOs of family life (that's Chief Operating Officer), I feel maxed out in both my time and money. This particular year I felt called to push past my own comfort and organize our church's Angel Tree project, a gift-giving program that matches local churches with children who have an incarcerated parent to buy gifts and offer encouragement. I was proud of myself for making this a priority in a month that felt full to the max. After all, if anything was important during Christmas, wasn't it this? Wasn't generous giving the very trait God modeled for us when he came so humbly as a baby in a manger? Wasn't this the Christmas spirit — to give when it wasn't convenient? So I created a spreadsheet.

A few days later I found myself at the store holding those last four ornaments that had been left on the tree. They held the names, ages and sizes of four teenage boys. Boys who wanted, or more likely needed, jeans and coats. In men's sizes. A few minutes into my shopping and I realized I was perturbed. Let me tell you — boys coats are expensive! And, well... boring to shop for. How did I get left with the most expensive gifts? Why didn't I get to buy teddy bears and toddler dresses? I should have chosen the baby dolls since I have girls myself AND was doing all the work. Our Christmas budget is already so tight — how will we possibly be able to afford these big kid items? I shouldn't have been so willing to take everything that was left. This isn't what I signed up for.

Oh how that hurt, to acknowledge what was going on inside my brain. Even worse, inside my heart. Hardly generous. Selfish would be the appropriate word, because I was giving to meet MY needs, not the needs of those boys whose names I held in my ungrateful hands. I pictured these boys with whose mothers and grandmothers I'd spoken. These were somebody's SONS. Other women had born them, cradled them, comforted them and likely still prayed for them. These were boys who had a parent in prison! And I was mad I needed to spend $20 more on each of them than the grandma next to me in the pew last Sunday?!

But here is what I found myself thinking: Twenty dollars is a lot to me these days. There are so many other people in our congregation who could easily give this. People who have teenage boys themselves, and this would be a teachable moment for those families, to have their sons give to boys their age. I know! For shame, right? A justification of why I shouldn't have to give.

I am not commanding you, but I want to test the sincerity of your love by comparing it with the earnestness of others. For you know the grace of our Lord Jesus Christ, that though he was rich, yet for your sake he became poor, so that you through his poverty might become rich." (2 Corinthians 8:8-9)

Here's the thing, when I stood in front of our congregation the Sunday before and explained the Angel Tree project to our church, and shared about my sweet conversations with these children's aunts and grandmothers, and about their simple wishes, I was getting something out of it. Recognition for a job well done. For using my gifts of communication and organization. Even for a beautifully decorated tree in the lobby. I wasn't thinking about the discomfort, or even pain, it might require of me.

God is so gentle with his words, "I am not commanding you." He just wants to see if you really are sincere in your faith. You say you love me, but are you willing to copy my behavior like I ask you to? Are you willing to give up one more stocking gift, or even five, for your own children, so others might have more? The "sincerity of my love" is what he is testing. And by the way — that sincerity is a choice. It may hurt, but it was my choice to give up some small comfort for the sake of people I may never meet. So that they may become rich.

Here's what I know: When I became a mother, when that first pregnancy test was positive, I gave with a selflessness I'd never known before. Without hesitation I gave up coffee and comfort and freedom and my body and a million other things, because I so intensely loved this person I hadn't yet met. And once she arrived, those sacrifices and that love just grew with each day. Sleep and dry breasts and concentration and uninterrupted adult conversations were all things of the past. So I know I have it in me. To love someone in the middle of the night when no one else is watching, when I want to cry because I'm so exhausted or I gag from the smell of the vomit I'm cleaning up or I simply want my bed to be my own. And I do it anyway. I push through anyway. And without thought of me, but of my kids whom I love with a fierceness I didn't know was in me.

Motherhood has given me a sense of the depth of generosity I can offer. But what about when it's not the people I love most dearly who need my generosity? God calls us to be generous to all of his children, not just the ones I call my own: Truly I tell you, whatever you did for one of the least of these brothers and sisters of mine, you did for me. (Matthew 25:40)

The least of these... Suddenly I am picturing four teenage boys with tough circumstances adorned in new, warm coats this Christmas. And giving until it hurts — makes a little more sense.

Questions

What does generosity look like to me?

How has motherhood made me more generous?

When have I been the recipient of a generous gift? How did that impact me?

What motivates me to be generous?

Is there anything that keeps me from stepping into generosity? What can I do about it?

Courage To Be a Neighbor

by Mandy Arioto

"Wherever you are, be all there." — Jim Elliott

I have a friend named Alma; she owns a business in downtown San Diego. It is a quaint little joint that people rent out for art shows and the occasional birthday party. She is no taller than five feet, has long, wavy, dark hair with gray streaks starting around her face, and the most beautiful blue eyes.

I saw Alma most every Sunday for the better part of a year, and each time we would chat about the neighborhood or about the renovations that she was making to her space. A few months after meeting, she shared her prized pozolé recipe with me. I knew after that that we had become friends.

I know a lot of things about Alma, partially because I ask a lot of questions but more importantly because she is so willing to share her life. She shared about her four kids, how she had never been married and how she had worked every day for the past 22 years in order to provide. One time she shared about how when she was younger and barely able to keep a roof over their head, she had done things that she wasn't proud of to feed her family.

She has lived life and has the stories to prove it.

What I learned from her, and so many other friends who I have met along the way, is that it is in the listening where friendship happens.

Listening is holy work. Real listening changes us. Because I believe that God puts people in our lives who are different than us for a reason. Instead of needing to be fixed, most of the time they just need to be loved.

Every one you will ever meet knows something you don't. So, when we listen and learn from one another we are participating in the holy. God's Kingdom come.

My friend Jen has a knack for turning people into family who have no blood relation to her. She knows every neighbor's name, and drops off cookies just because. Jen has the gift of proximity. Just being around her makes you feel more like yourself.

I am working on being more like Jen. Especially with the people who live next door and on my street. The people who are breathing and eating not even 50 feet away from me on a daily basis. For some weird reason it is easier for me to become friends with people I meet at the grocery store than it is with the people who live next door to me. But I think proximity matters, so we are making an effort as a family to get to know the individuals with whom we share our street.

Here are a few things we are trying out in order to be better neighbors:

Instead of having a garage sale we are having a garage giveaway. We are putting all of our extra stuff out on the front yard with a sign that says, "take what you need." We want to be better sharers, and the truth is that we have stuff that other people need. Giving it away is an excellent family share opportunity — and a worthy swap for the few bucks we would've made.

I have had to get over my house. I live in a teeny tiny house. It is cozy and messy. My kids love art projects, which means that there is sure to be glitter in my carpets. This makes me pause before inviting people over. Then I remind myself about the times that I have enjoyed myself the most at a friend's house. Was it because they had the biggest or nicest house and they were gourmet cooks. Nope. What made me love being there the most was that I felt loved. This gives me confidence to pack out my tiny house, serve the leftover lasagna and love my neighbors like crazy.

Additionally, our house is open to all the kids in the neighborhood. And man, can I tell you they eat an insane amount of snacks. Our kids sometimes complain that the little kids from next door come over and pick their noses, but what they are learning is that relationships aren't always neat and easy.

We are by no means perfect at this neighboring business. But what we are realizing is that when Jesus tells us to "Love God and love our neighbors as ourselves," maybe the neighbors he is talking about are our actual next-door neighbors.

Real security comes from a feeling of interconnectedness. It means removing barriers by asking questions. A realization that we are all in this together. So I have decided that I don't need to have all the answers. Instead, I want to be a friend who shares my snacks with the lady sitting next to me on the subway. The one who has weary eyes and who might feel like some Lays potato chips just might save her. Then we will talk about all the cool and hard stuff we're experiencing and learn that we are more alike than we might have originally thought. We will be neighbors.

So, don't worry if you can't cook or your house isn't as fancy pants as someone else's. Just invite someone over, and listen deeply.

Oh, and deliver cookies just because. Everybody will love you if you show up with cookies.

Questions

What qualities do I expect in a friend? Who are the five people I count as my closest friends?

Who are my oldest friends? Why have we remained friends for so long?

Who are my newest friends? How did we meet? What are the qualities that caused me to

seek and maintain their friendship?

Do I want to broaden my group of friends or am I happy with just those I have now?

If I were to ask my good friends, what would they tell me are the qualities they value in me?

What would they say makes me a good friend? Do I live up to my own definition of what a

good friend should be? Are there aspects of my personality that I would like to work on so

that I could be a better friend? What are they?

Are there problems that seem to crop up for me in friendship after friendship?

Who are my neighbors?

Courage To Try

by Mandy Arioto

"There will be a few times in your life when all your instincts will tell you to do something, something that defies logic, upsets your plans, and may seem crazy to others. When that happens, you do it. Listen to your instincts and ignore everything else. Ignore logic, ignore the odds, ignore the complications, and just go for it." — Judith McNaught

My roommate in college once told me that the way you spend New Year's will be how you spend the rest of the year. I wish that were true, because if it were I would spend the entire week leading up to December 31 choreographing the most epic night ever. It would be sprinkled with sequins and filled with loved ones. And I would be assured that my year was brimming with all of the adventure, celebration and chocolate that I could pack into a six-hour evening. My entire year determined in a few hours. Epic.

Instead, I was snuggled under the covers at 9 p.m. on New Year's Eve and had spent the last month trying to muster some inspiration. A plan that will give shape to the next twelve months. I don't really believe in resolutions because they are too predictable. We all want to exercise enough that we can throw our Spanx in the trash, to feed our kids healthy food for every meal, to start our Etsy shop with crafts that we made from recycled trash that people will want to buy for hundreds of dollars each (OK, that might just be me). We want to feel passionate and alive, to laugh more and worry less. We want to move with purpose.

It seems to me that our DNA is engrained with a need to move forward. You see this right from the beginning. I have never had to encourage any of my babies to crawl. With every fiber of their being they were struggling to move. First to roll, and then to crawl, and then to walk. And the whole process is filled with danger. There are bumped heads and bruises. But when they choose to pick themselves up in spite of the falls, they eventually learn to run.

God created us for progress. No one grows up hoping that someday they'll be ordinary. Instead, the frustrating reality is that each and every one of us has been created with a drive to move, to become something better — something more than we already are.

Often our dreams are stuck in our heads. Ideas held together by duct tape and some days. How do we move from the idea that compels us, to actually doing something about it? This is where we get stuck.

That's why I am convinced that the only way to move is to make the transition from head to hands. Because the truth is, sometimes there is magic in our lives and sometimes there isn't. Sometimes there are signs to point us in the right direction and sometimes we have to do the pointing ourselves.

That is when we just have to try.

And keep trying.

Do you have a try that is beckoning to you?

Me and my girlfriends call it "your thing."

It is the thing that keeps showing up in your life, an opportunity that is just waiting for you to choose it. Something that inspires you and makes you feel more alive. Maybe it is traveling, or starting a business, maybe it is going back to school.

If you're like me, there are things you can see that other people can't. Like you know a story needs to be shared or a product could be better, you know that there is an injustice that needs a champion. Maybe that is your thing. The nuances of our try-lists don't matter; what is important is that we push our boundaries and muster the courage to simply start.

Here are a few truths I have learned about trying from the smartest people I know:

If you wait to try until you feel ready, you'll never get around to it. The best time to start is right now. Don't wait for the stars to align and Jesus to appear before you with a sign that says 'today is your day'. Your very breath means that you were put here today to do something. Get a jump start on the future and go for it.

If you have an idea of what you are supposed to try, of what you were put here to do, then just go and do that. And if you don't have your specific thing then don't worry about it, don't overthink it, just start the next right thing. Then after that, things will start happening. Things that perhaps have God's fingerprint on them.

If you don't know how to start, ask someone who does. You will be amazed by the people who want to help you — you just have to ask.

Trying isn't just about starting something new. It's about living outside of your head. Becoming congruent with the person you are and the person you want to be. Don't be so focused on what is, be more concerned about who you are becoming through the process.

And do you know what the truth is? None of this is as big or scary as it feels.

Sometimes I psych myself out. I convince myself that this is not the time in my life to start something. That this raising three little kids/working mom/wife season of life is the time to play it small and safe.

Confession time. There are a lot of things that keep me from trying, but do you want to know the most embarrassing one? It's ABC. Or more specifically, ABC's *The Bachelor* or *The Bachelorette,* depending on the season.

For whatever reason it is infinitely easier to camp out on my couch to watch other women date ridiculous men while sipping tea under my most favorite cozy blanket than it is to start writing the book that my heart has been dreaming about.

That and the fact that starting is risky.

It takes courage to take the first step because the truth is — you might fail. You might hate what you started or decide that you started one thing when it really should have been something entirely different that you gave your efforts to. You might even face rejection from strangers — or worse — people who know and love you.

The remarkable thing about life is that it is a forever try.

Sometimes your internal warning system will steer you the wrong way. Your mind will tangle up your body and convince you that it isn't worth trying. That you don't have what it takes — so why bother starting? This initial resistance happens to all of us, the trick is not to pretend that the resistance doesn't exist — it's simply to refuse to let fear make your decisions for you.

Our fears will never disappear. Each day brings new anxieties or the return of old ones, but also new opportunities to overcome them. Sometimes it means one step. One step in a new direction. We aren't talking marathons here people. Maybe it is more like a run down the driveway. And then tomorrow you can go a little farther. The most important thing is simply to start. Soon you will be able to look back and see how far you have come, but for now, just put on your running shoes.

You have been placed here, in this time and space, with unique abilities. Made to try a lot of things, to love some and to let some go. So make some mistakes. Start some things and fail miserably at them. Because if you are making mistakes, it means that you are trying — trying new things, learning, risking yourself, and changing your world. So make gloriously embarrassing mistakes. Make mistakes nobody's ever made before. Don't worry that it isn't good enough, or it isn't perfect. Trying is a holy endeavor.

After God formed humanity out of the dust of the earth he whispered in our ear, "It's your try," and now all of eternity is waiting to see what you will do with your life.

So, whatever it is you're scared of doing ...
Starting a conversation ... Starting a business ...
Starting to get help ... Starting to pray ...
Whatever your thing is ...
You have totally got this.
Take a risk.
Try.

Questions

Do I have "a thing"? Am I doing my thing? If not, what's keeping me from it?

When I think about starting something new, how do I feel?

Is there something that in ten years I will wish I would have started today?

What is one thing I can do this week to try?

Courage To Be Intentional

by Alexandra Kuykendall

"Only she who attempts the absurd can achieve the impossible." — Dr. Linda Brodsky

"I wanted you to learn a foreign language while you were still little." My mother's answer to why she packed me up when I was eight and moved me from Seattle to Italy. Furniture stored. Boxes packed. Passports renewed. And we were on our way. "When I started studying languages in college, I learned the younger you are when you start, the easier it is. I decided then I wanted my kids to learn another language when they were still young and it was still easy."

Years before my mother became a mother she decided on a value she wanted to pass on. Compounded with her own professional experience of teaching adults English as a Second Language and her knack for living around the world, she was intentional about making it happen. Even when it wasn't convenient or easy. And her attempt to pass on a love of languages to her only child worked. That daughter went on to be a Spanish major just like her mother a whole generation down the turn.

And when that Spanish major, who had spent her childhood envisioning taking her own family globetrotting as part of their lifestyle, fell in love with a man who'd grown up to be the third generation to live on the same piece of land, and had never considered foreign living as one of his values — the two had to come to peace. He said, "We can consider it when the time comes." She said, "We can make sure we bring the world to our children." And then they were married, and one of their bigger differences was put off to deal with later ... you know — when they had kids.

A few years of nesting down the road and the first baby comes and then the second. And that mother begins to wonder how she is doing in that commitment she made to herself. How is she bringing the world to her children? The truth was she had surrounded herself with people whose lives, cultures and languages looked a lot like her own. The value behind the globetrotting life, to show and experience the differences God created on the planet with his people, was not happening. And she had to ask herself, "Why?" If she held on to this value so dearly, why wasn't she making it happen?

Because it wasn't easy.

Okay, so we all know this mom was me. And I confess when I gravitate toward people, they tend to be people whose lives look a lot like mine. Kids? Then I don't have to explain to you my generally disheveled state. Married? Then you get my steady, but perhaps drama-free (aka excitement-free) love life. And fill in other details about my life: work part-time, city dweller, church attender, and mom of four. And the closer a person resembles these details, well — the more likely they are to be like me. And the easier it is for us to have a relationship because there is so much I don't have to explain. A person like me just gets certain parts of me without me even having to explain. And life is complicated enough without having to explain everything all the time.

So how does that fit in with a personal dream of exposing my kids to the larger world when my most comfortable version of life is pretty narrow? Enter intentionality. That spot where I must choose to be in relationships that feel more awkward than others, even though understanding and authenticity will take work, and won't always come easily.

Over the years my husband Derek and I have made some decisions with intentionality that in some cases have come quite naturally, and made us feel comfortable. But some cases have required trust on our parts, because they've pushed against our natural tendencies. The neighborhood we live in, the public schools we send our kids to (in that neighborhood we chose), the career calling Derek has answered serving our city's homeless. All expose our kids (and me and Derek, too) to people whose lives actually do look pretty different than ours. The languages they speak at home, the food they eat, the places they spend their free time, their family structures... all different than ours. Does this look like the globe trekking dreams of my youth? With my kids riding the trains through Europe like I did? Or serving the poor in the Southern Hemisphere like my idealistic college-self pictured? No. I have friends who are living both of these versions of my dreams with their kids. I depend on Facebook to keep me updated on their travels and to take these adventures vicariously. But do my kids know families from around the world? Yes. Do they see us serving the poor here at home? Yes. Our intentionality brings out the values Derek and I want to instill in our girls, but he and I both have to flex on what exactly that looks like.

My own MOPS group is a place where this plays out. Despite my tendency toward introversion, I often force myself to open up in my MOPS group for this very reason. It makes me interact with women whose lives are different than mine, and that is good for me. We are all moms, yes. But our lives outside of MOPS are all over the place as far as what they look like. And we love each other through those differences. Have there been awkward conversations? Sometimes. Has there been uncomfortable silence? Yes. Do I know these other moms love me even if my marriage, mothering, work life is drastically different than theirs? Yes. And I pray they feel the same acceptance from me. Without a doubt, they give me a new and fresh perspective on my problems, stressors, worries, joys, celebrations and milestones. They remind me how wonderful and unique my life really is.

My mother held onto a value that she cherished, and spun the globe to make it happen and to take me with her. Sometimes I feel like I'm copping out on my own version of her adventures. But then I remember that living with intention is about the underlying desired outcome. The root of my hopes for my kids to experience the world is to see differences can be good, and that diversity makes life interesting and rich. That we don't have to be afraid of what is different, but can learn from it and even learn to love it. God has created people that are his image bearers, even though they look completely different from each other, and more importantly from us. I'm trying to push toward these values right where I am. To be intentional where I am planted.

Questions

What things did I want to be intentional about in parenting before I had kids?

Have I been true to these dreams? What has allowed me to keep or break these promises to myself?

How am I intentional in my parenting? In other areas of my life?

How can I continue to be intentional, even when it is difficult?

Do I give myself permission to change my mind about what my dreams look like? Why or why not?

Courage To Find Significance in The Everyday

by Mandy Arioto

"I don't think life is absurd. I think we are all here for a huge purpose. I think we shrink from the immensity of the purpose we are here for." — Norman Mailer

We all know as moms that we would do anything for our kids. But today I truly took one for my team. I crawled under the door of a public restroom because my five year old daughter insisted on going in the stall by herself, which of course meant locking the door. She yelled to me that she needed help, which is not easily accomplished when mom is on the other side of the locked door and said child will not hop off the potty to unlock the door. After what seemed like hours of negotiations, the only alternative was to crawl under the stall door. That's right, hands and knees on the floor followed by soldier crawl on my tummy under the door to find my five year old smiling at me from her perch on the potty.

Hours later I contemplate my other options that I didn't think of at the time. I could have crawled over the stall. A bit precarious but certainly more sanitary that the floor crawl that I hastily chose as my only option.

And as we drove home, my kids happily singing along to some adorable and obnoxious kid CD, all I could think was, "This is what my life has come to. Crawling around on public restroom floors."

If I am expert on any subject, I think ordinariness might be it. As a mother of three kids, ordinary is my jam. It is the rhythm to my day, the drum beat that gives cadence to my life.

When I am being completely honest with you I will tell you that while ordinary is my metronome, I have often struggled to find meaning within its constant repetition.

Throughout my twelve years of raising kids I have worked full-time, sometimes in the home and sometimes outside of it. And because we are all girlfriends and can trust each other with real feelings, I will admit that it hasn't been my work in marketing that has been the most challenging part of my day. Rather, it has been the everyday chores of scrubbing dishes and managing bedtime that have proven to test my fortitude. And it is not because these tasks are difficult but rather because I find I am more susceptible to label them as insignificant.

And I don't think I am alone. I know so many people who despise their ordinary existence and think that their life does not have much significance unless they are performing Facebook-worthy acts.

We live in a time and a culture that celebrates the extraordinary, yet so much of life is made up of the mundane. Routine and repetition fill most moments.

I can't help but feel that our quest for efficiency has stolen life from us, taken our ability to see the beauty in the mundane.

I wonder if it is time to make more room for the ordinary.

After all, most of my daily tasks are not exercises in productivity. Doing laundry that will need to be washed again in two days, cooking a meal, reading a bedtime story are far from efficient but they are beautiful gifts that I give to the people with whom I share my best moments.

Too often, I compartmentalize my life into segments that matter and segments that don't. Like taking cookies to the old couple across the street matters, and doing the laundry doesn't. This kind of thinking leaves me scrambling to check the things off of my to-do list that don't matter so that I can get to the things that really do. However, my system is broken.

I know this because every once in a while something happens — something that would never show up on a to-do list. Something mundane and completely revolutionary like my 5 year old snuggling up to my side and kissing my forehead. And I realize, "This moment gives meaning to my entire existence as a human being."

This simple moment helps to remind me that I don't need to strive to make the ordinary things profound, they already are. The question becomes: Do I have the eyes to see them?

I am coming to learn the truth in the Celtic proverb, milking the cow is holy. It acknowledges that it all matters. Everyday moments are profound. Making dinner is holy. Doing the dishes is holy. Reading my kids bedtime stories is just as significant as when I am preparing to speak to a crowd of strangers. If we do the simple tasks from a loving heart, then we will always be participating in something significant.

And all the plain things, the things that make up the routines of a day, like a spoon in oatmeal, an open book, toys on the floor, those things comprise holy moments. Especially when we have eyes to see the story, mystery and beauty of the moment.

So friends, I have an idea: let's reclaim the everyday. Let's name it sacred.

And let's be brave enough to call bathroom floors and bedtimes significant.

May you find wonder in ordinary time.
May you relish the warmth of holding hands and the joy of tasting treats.
May you be present in what you do.
May you see that each small task is worthy of your best.
May tasks that normally burden be filled with life-giving meaning.
And may you see that the work of your day is significant.

Questions

What is the current rhythm of my day?

What is keeping me from finding the significance in my day-to-day life?

What are five moments from today that are seared in my memory as significant?

What is one thing I can do this week to find the significance in my daily routine?

Courage To Face Your Real Mom Fears

by Sherry Surratt

"All of us have moments in our lives that test our courage. Taking children into a house with a white carpet is one of them." — Erma Bombeck

I remember bringing our first child, Mike, home from the hospital. I was sore, I was exhausted, and to be honest I was scared to death. What was it the nurses had told me about sterilizing the bottle nipples? What if I couldn't get him to stop crying? What in the world was I supposed to do with that funny looking nasal syringe?

Within the first few days these questions led to even deeper ones. Would I ever get any sleep? What in the world was going on with my saggy looking body? Would things ever settle back into what felt normal for Geoff and I and our schedules and routines? Would I ever have fun again? I began to feel guilty for even having these thoughts. What kind of a mom worries about herself when she's just had the most beautiful baby boy in the world?

The more I thought about these questions, the more depressed I got. I began to feel sad and anxious, and throughout my thoughts one central question kept swirling around: Do I have what it takes to be a good enough mom? I had this picture of a world class, got-it-all-together mom in my head, and she didn't look anything like me. She was confident. She had the answers. She never left the house without a perfectly organized designer diaper bag, armed with enough diapers, wipes and snacks for the whole neighborhood. Nope, this wasn't me. I remember standing in Walmart frantically searching for a simple wipe in my bag and finding one lone shoe. It was mine.

As the years went by, I was able to answer the question about being a good enough mom with a yes, but I realized my reality was far from my picture of that perfect, confident mom. While my children never left the house naked or starving, I made mistakes. I didn't always have patience. Sometimes I made dumb decisions. I worried and wasted many anxious hours thinking up 'what if?' scenarios that never happened. I swallowed down a lot of fear and pretended it wasn't there.

Over the last year, I've been pondering a different question: What does a brave mom look like? I think the answer starts with admitting what she's not. She doesn't pretend to not have fear. She doesn't just power through, giving the impression that she's got everything under control. She's not a got-it all-together supermom.

As I've talked with many ages and stages of moms about this concept of mom fear, a different picture of brave has brought clarity for me. A brave mom is someone who is courageous enough to be real. She admits what's scary and what she worries about. She exposes it to the light of truth and doesn't ruminate on the fear itself, but seeks help and solutions.

I recently talked with Amy, a mom of four who said she has dealt with the fear that something bad will happen to her children, like being in a car accident or being snatched by a stranger in a public place. She said the fear has kept her up at night, caused her anxiety as she's loaded her kids in the car and led her to develop a frantic obsession to never take her eyes or hands off of her children when they leave the house. Amy is not alone. Research tells us that this is one of the top mom fears and stretches universally across moms of preschoolers and older children. But Amy said she now feels this fear has taken its proper place in her life, and no longer makes her miserable. I asked her how.

She said she focused on the following strategy: Name it, Learn it, Do it, Let it go. She started by admitting what the fear was and put it in a sentence. I'm afraid my children will get hurt. She then focused on learning about the dangers that concerned her most and tried to apply the facts to how reasonable her fears were. She found out that the percentage of children getting injured in car accidents has gone down drastically over the years due to improved car seats and child restraint laws, and that incidences of child abduction have dropped dramatically over the past ten years due to heightened awareness and legal enforcement. She read blogs, did Internet research and talked with family and friends. She noted the things that she could do to impact her children's safety, like staying diligent with seat belts and good car seats, and talking to her kids about common sense rules with strangers. Though she couldn't eliminate the dangers completely, she focused on the things she could control, and then she did a beautiful thing: she let it go. She said she pictured her fear as a balloon that got lighter and lighter each time she focused on something she could do that would make a difference, and then she released the string and let it float up, up and away.

I declare Amy's strategy brilliant! She didn't pretend or try to talk herself out of it. She faced it, educated herself and then took action. After doing everything she could, she allowed herself to be free from the fear and step into her new brave reality, admitting that there are scary things out there but refusing to let them control her.

So how about you? Are there mom fears that shut you down? I still deal with mom fear and worry (I think I always will), but in addition to applying Amy's strategy, I also have a go-to Bible verse that I lean into:

When I am afraid, I put my trust in you. (Psalm 56:3)

The 'you' in this verse is God, and if you deal with fear as a mom, God is calling your name. David, the writer of this verse, admits freely here that he deals with fear, and it's OK for us to admit it as well. God not only understands, he's here to help. As we lean into him, he provides us with the peace of knowing he's in control. As we dive into his word (the Bible), he reminds us we are not alone, even as a mom. He gave us the children we have and in doing so, he made us the exact right mom for our kids. We don't have to be perfect. God made us to be enough.

Questions

What's my biggest fear as a mom? Is this fear more about me as a mom, or the safety and well-being of my child? Where do I think this fear comes from?

Are there any circumstances or times when I deal with fear the most? Do I see any patterns or things that might trigger it? If so, what can I learn from this?

Do I have a friend or mentor I can go to for encouragement and prayer when life seems really scary? If not, who is one mom or mentor in my MOPS group I can talk to?

Want to hear from other moms who struggle with fear and how they overcome it? Read *Brave Mom: Facing and Overcoming Your Real Mom Fears*, our new MOPS Theme book, coming Sept 2014.

Courage To Be Broken

by Alexandra Kuykendall

"Until you are broken, you don't know what you're made of." — Melissa Molomo

My 5-month-old baby lay in the hospital bed, hooked up to oxygen to keep her bitty lungs from working too hard. It was okay, I knew she was in good hands, and I'd been here before. I had moments when I was able to reassure myself with such words. My eldest daughter Gabi, this baby's biggest sis, had been hospitalized with the same RSV as an infant years earlier. I knew this story. I had lived it once before.

But then the words of affirmation I tried to tell and retell myself were overtaken by the harsh reality of the moment. The glare of the hospital floor, the cold that I couldn't shake, the hospital crib that felt like a cage. When I put the sides down I could crawl in and snuggle with Gracie when the nurses weren't around. I felt small... and inadequate... and so very less than.

I didn't understand all of the medical terms, and I felt like I wasn't the take-charge mom I should have been. I worried I was somehow neglecting my other sick children at home — didn't they need me, too? My mothering insecurities were swirling around me at hurricane levels. Was I really vigilant enough about the germs in our house? I hadn't taken her to the doctor soon enough. My own childhood asthma was the genetic predisposer that put Gracie and her sisters at risk of chronic respiratory issues in the first place.

In that hospital room, when I was doing everything I possibly could to comfort my baby, I felt like the world's biggest failure as a mother.

There is courage in admitting I don't have it all together. In motherhood I fall short in so many ways. But some of those ways are much easier to confess. I don't know what's for dinner, my house is a disaster, I yelled at my kids today. But what about those deeper insecurities? I'm not cut out for this — some days I just want to pull out of the driveway and leave. I really shouldn't be trusted with other people's well-being. I lay beside my daughter in that hospital room feeling like the doctor's questions were directed at me, because somehow I was to blame for this whole situation.

I was deep in the heart of self doubt.

And it is here, in this place of "I simply can't do this," that I must seek courage. Courage to recognize that I am limited by what is humanly possible. Courage to acknowledge that what I bring to the table is one broken mess of a woman.

It takes courage to say not only do I not have it all together, but also it is impossible for me to ever truly have it all together, because I am human.

God's story of creation centers around the fact that this world is not as it should be. God created beauty and people, and then evil entered and messed up the whole plan. The rest of history has been the story of us — you and me and the woman down the block and all of our ancestors since time immemorial — figuring out how to live in the mess. A broken world filled with broken people. And I am one of them.

In that hospital room, I felt all of my human limitations throbbing. I hadn't slept well in days as I cared for a house full of sick kids, followed by a few nights of sleep in a hospital where day and night have no distinction. I was emotionally exhausted as I texted babysitters and my mother-in-law and my husband special instructions for the other two at home, and I was flat out worried for my sweet baby with oxygen tubes up her nose and an IV in her tiny arm. It was easy in that moment to fully surrender that I am broken and not enough.

It is months later, with healthy kids and soccer practice and preschool parties in full swing, that I must continue to have the courage to say I'm broken.

On the days when I can pull off the façade of a well-lived, well-organized, well-planned life, it is harder to admit that I walk around with a fractured heart. This crack down the middle of my spirit is in part because I've lived in this broken world and been let down, hurt, lied to and unfriended. But all of those experiences are symptoms of the larger issue that we as people are broken. Me included — no matter how well I'm able to pretend to be in control. I practice embracing my brokenness in the following ways:

I recognize the gifts. My life is overflowing with wonderful gifts — a husband I love to be with, kids who can run and jump and speak, and a warm home in a place that sees cold nights. When I acknowledge that the majority of the good things in my life are not of my own making — simply gifts I didn't earn — I consider my own brokenness and I am grateful.

I choose my friends wisely. I have no time for competitive friendships. Warning signs of this kind of relationship include trying to prove my worth through my paycheck, my kids' accomplishments or how my house looks. I find it much more helpful to be around people who show their ugly openly. This kind of vulnerability reminds me that we are all broken, and gives me permission to be authentic.

I examine my expectations. Why am I stressed about making the class Valentines cute? About wearing the right thing to the party? About having an amazing summer bucket list? Where do these self-imposed standards come from? I remind myself that there will always be more I can do, but I am broken and it's okay to do simply what I can.

I remember how the world actually is. As opposed to how I would like it to be. Since evil entered, the world has been messed up. My imperfect, human state is a result of that. So many of my minutes are spent trying to make my life what I think it should be, striving for unattainable perfection. When I remember that we all share in this brokenness, I feel the courage to embrace that identity.

Questions

Does the world seem a broken place to me? Why or why not?

What brokenness and I trying to hide from myself? From others?

What stops me from letting my "ugly" show — from being truly authentic in my relationships?

Courage To Risk

by Mandy Arioto

"Do one thing every day that scares you." — Eleanor Roosevelt

The sun is chasing the darkness as the sky turns turquoise. I have been up since before the sunrise in order to make it to the summit. I am standing at the edge of a cable ladder, suspended 8,000 feet above the Yosemite Valley almost to the summit of Half Dome. Creed is belting out "With Arms Wide Open" on a radio that a fellow climber has sitting on the ground next to him (it was the early 2000s — don't judge me). In the background a handful of people are waiting for their chance on the cables. It is a 400-foot vertical climb, and the cables are filled with climbers steadily making their way to the summit. It is the only way to the top, and I wonder, "Is this safe?"

The first time I attempted the climb to the summit, I froze. I was playing out every possible horrible scenario in my mind and the mental gymnastics that I was engaged in were convincing me that it was too scary. Every muscle in my body stopped firing and I froze. Unable to move, I resigned myself to simply breathing. So I parked myself on a flat rock at the base of the ladder and watched climber after climber make the first move toward summit. My husband Joe was with me, waiting patiently and trying to be supportive. He knew how much I would regret not making the climb.

What is it about youth that makes risk more palatable? When we are young, adventure is our currency. Stories are built and lives are shared around our risks. But as we get older, we become fearful of leaving the comfort of our habits. Reason woos us. What once enticed us as adventurous now feels dangerous in its unpredictability.

Breaking this pattern means foregoing our routines in order to conquer a challenge. Risk breathes wonder into our souls, reminding us that we can handle anything. For me, on this particular day, it meant attempting to climb a mountain.

After sitting with me for a half hour as I tried to muster my courage, Joe said, "You're waiting to not be afraid, and that's never going to happen. If you want this, you're going to have to climb even though you are afraid."

It took me 20 minutes to muster up the courage to risk.

A girl who is waiting (quite impatiently) behind me insists I start to climb or get off the cables. Without thinking, I stick out my arms and grab hold of the ladder. And I climb. Risking is not about the mountain before us. It's about freeing ourselves from our preconceived limits.

I really dislike doing dishes. I don't know why. I would rather do eleven loads of laundry and vacuum the whole house than do one sink full of dishes. My husband always jokes with me that household chores would be so much easier if I didn't care about safety. See, I refuse to use all of those dangerous household chemicals. Instead I use all-natural, non-chemical cleaning products like baking soda and peroxide.

Almost every bottle of cleaning product in our house is relatively safe. Except for one bottle. This one bottle is the type of cleaner that has a skeleton face emblem on the front with the words DANGER in huge letters. This is the bottle that my husband Joe busts out when it is his turn to clean. He uses it because it works. Like — really well, and really quickly. Instead of scrubbing, all he has to do is spray it on and let it sit. Whereas I have to scrub over and over with my safe cleaning products.

One day, as Joe witnessed me trying to scrub the kitchen sink clean with my arsenal of safe cleaning products, he said, "You know, sometimes dangerous is better."

Isn't that so true? And this is bigger than cleaning supplies, isn't it? The same thing is true of God. He is Divine and He is Dangerous and there is nothing safe about Him. He is a God who calls us to risk our lives on Him, asking us to do things that don't seem to make sense. Our choice becomes to entrust our lives to the dangerous God or to play it safe on the sidelines. Choosing to follow Jesus becomes an act of risky adventure.

Mark Batterson puts it beautifully when he writes in his book, *Wild Goose Chase* (Multnomah, 2008), "It seems to me that God is always calling us into terra incognita — unknown or unexplored territory. That is where risk begins and adventure is found. To follow Him, we need to be willing to go somewhere we have never been."

Along the edge of almost every medieval map you will find the words terra incognita. Cartographers put it there to warn of the unknown. In addition to the label, they would draw two-headed dragons in the uncharted portions of the map. The dragons were a warning, a visual representation of internal feelings. They stated the fact that the unknown was fiercely terrifying. In fact tales surfaced about what would happened if you risked exploring. Common belief was that you would fall off the edge of the earth, that bravery would lead to inevitable doom. But the fact is, that new worlds were discovered because a few brave-hearted ones slayed the two-headed dragons of fear.

After all, have you ever admired someone because they were cautious? I have never once heard someone list 'careful' as an attribute that they admired in another person. It is quite the opposite. We love writers who risk honesty. People who risk their own safety to bring food to starving children. Women who risk welcoming another woman's child into their families to raise them as their own. The ones who stare fear in the face and act in spite of it — those are our heroes.

Friend, is it possible that God is calling you to risk bigger than you have ever imagined? Is the spirit of God pleading with you to stop settling for the status quo? Is this your moment to risk big?

And in the very wise words of Creed front man Scott Strapp (like I said earlier, don't judge me),

"I hope he understands
That he can take this life
And hold it by the hand
And he can greet the world
With arms wide open."

May God breathe into your soul the beauty of traveling outside of your comfort zone.

May adventure be a lighthouse drawing you nearer to your own courage.

May your map be filled with uncharted frontiers,

And may you have the courage to climb.

Questions

What is the biggest risk I have ever taken?

Is there an area of life where I am being too careful?

What is God whispering to my soul about risk?

Is there something in particular that I need to do this week to stare fear in the face and act in spite of it?

What is one thing I can do this week to take a risk?

Courage To Tell Your Story

by Alexandra Kuykendall

"Either write something worth reading or do something worth writing." — Benjamin Franklin

I placed one foot in front of the other, grateful the library staircase was long. Every step was a crossing over from my everyday life of a nursing baby and school drop-offs and work emails into a few hours of writing. Once inside, my feet took me on autopilot to my spot on the second floor, the window that looked across the commons onto the chapel with the cross.

But first I had to walk between bookshelves.

Rows of books written by people who believed enough in the topics at hand that they gave hours of life to pound out the words. It was a repeated daily passage into the physical, emotional and spiritual space of writing down my story. I walked through the aisles, past the authors who had gone before me, trusting if they could do it, I could too.

Once at my desk with a view, my laptop out and my coffee waiting to be finished, I read an email. From my mother-in-law, a seasoned writer, who sent me almost daily encouragements as I tried to type my soul out, story by story, line by line, word by word. Her email included a blog post written by a writer for which she and I shared an admiration: Donald Miller. She loved his emphasis on story and I admired his honesty. This particular post was entitled "The Best Writing Advice I've Ever Received." And this writer who I admired oh so much simply said he was divinely nudged with the phrase, "Love your reader."

Love. Your. Reader.

You, who I pictured sitting across that library table from me sharing some coffee and conversation. You, a listener willing to hear the details of my own journey, deserved to be loved as I told them. I loved through the particulars that I thought you needed to hear. The ones that talked of a broken heart as a girl, searching for significance in all the places a girl would, of a young woman falling in love and the fear in it, and midnight marriage prayers only a few years later. Of motherhood and all of its expectations and waves of emotion that I wasn't prepared for. I told of the questions, the doubts — because I wanted you to know you are not alone. I wanted to love you.

And if your story is not to be written, but to be spoken out loud, the premise is still love your listener. Because the courage to be vulnerable through the "this happened to me" and "I felt this" is giving someone else the freedom to say, "me too." To sigh that huge exhale of relief that she is not alone in the experiences and feelings of this mixed-up and sometimes backward life.

And how interesting this phrasing — love your reader — when the whole premise of my story, of all of our stories, is love. Three burning questions that get to the core of who we are: Am I lovable? Am I loved? Am I loving? When I consider what truly defines me, it is Love. The Love-Giver, who gave his very self on the cross. Who CHOSE to take on the worst of the world in order to heal it. To heal us. For God is love.

And yet so much of my journey is confusing that love. Is looking for validation that yes I am lovable, and that please, please love me kind of ask, and the failing after failing of loving the people around me well. These doubts make me want to edit my story in the telling in case anyone might be turned off. Only when I look at The Artist's truth and ask, *Am I lovable? Am I loved? Am I loving?*, do I get a proper sense of my worth. He tells me his Grace covers it all. I don't have to be everything, or enough, he is enough. I can rest in his pure and generous love. The Artist's Daughter.

And it is within this freedom of the gift of grace, pure love, that I can boldly tell my story. That I did in book form. I had it all in my heart as it was now my turn to pound out those words. Because I believed in the topic at hand, that grace is given and it is enough. Because I loved you.

The courage to tell a story is the courage to go back into that moment and relive it, but now with the vantage point of time and understanding. And when we do — when we tell each other our stories and do it with the fresh eyes of who we are today — we take back some control in how we understand the events.

But what if we don't have perspective today? What if we are in the middle of the unfolding story right now? Or the ending we dreaded actually happened and doesn't get easier with time? Real and valid questions. The mystery of our stories when we have to ask, "Where was God when....?" Or "Where is he now?" For me, these are the stories that require more courage. Because they are the stories that aren't tied up with a pretty bow at the end. They are funky and wild and mysterious. And they are real.

In fact, when I've listened to others' stories, those of addiction and missteps and survival, that's when I've heard the truth-tellers. The level of drama and intrigue isn't what has captured me, we are all dished different doses of those. It's the honesty, and the courage required to speak such honesty, that grips me and causes me to lean in to hear more. It's the kind of story sharing I think Jesus calls us to when he tells us to speak boldly. He sent out the twelve closest to him, those Disciples, to do great things in the world. And he said

> "Don't be intimidated. Eventually everything is going to be out in the open, and everyone will know how things really are. So don't hesitate to go public now."
> — Matthew 10:26-27, The Message

It's this kind of story telling that has been a gift to me because it gives me a new kind of perspective — a shared life understanding. Even more it offers me freedom to say this life is difficult, or nearly impossible. The "I'm not sure I can make it another day" and the "I still don't understand why this happened" gives me the freedom to rip my pretty bows off the tops of my stories too. To say, "here it is, my life in the midst." With some exhilarating, tender, purely beautiful parts. And some unfolding, uncertain, insecure parts. My story is a mix of both.

Part of my story is the redeemed part, and part is waiting for the redemption. Sometimes my going public is with my husband or my bestie and sometimes it's with a big group. But I know this: that God doesn't want our stories to be hidden, he wants them to be shared — so we can see life as it really is, and hopefully God as he really is.

Questions

Does telling my story feel intimidating in any way? If so, why? If not, why not?

How do time and perspective help me understand my story?

What about my story makes it uniquely mine?

When has hearing someone else's story given me freedom?

Why might God want me to share my story rather than keep it hidden?

Courage To Be Passionate

by Mandy Arioto

"There is no passion to be had in playing small — in settling for a life less than the one you are capable of living." — Nelson Mandela

Last Saturday night the stars aligned in our universe. The children who live in our house, the womb-mates as we affectionately refer to them, were each invited to various sleepovers. Three kids. Three sleepovers. ON THE SAME NIGHT.

Miraculous.

Time for a date night. We went to a fancy-schmancy romantic restaurant that Joe found, played truth or dare in said fancy-schmancy restaurant, spent more money on dinner than we should have, and breathed and talked and held hands as we left.

It was perfect.

The importance of focusing on us, just him and me, is obvious. But truthfully it is sometimes lost on me. I like hanging with my kids. It's pricey to book a babysitter, and sometimes it feels like a lot of effort to get out of the house. In other words I am really lame occasionally. Can I add one more excuse to the mix? We just moved (nine months ago) and have had the hardest time finding a babysitter we trust. Whew, that is a lot of excuses. I told you, lame.

But Saturday we had no excuses — so we dated. And it helped me to remember that experiencing life without kids from time to time is essential. It is a reminder that we're more than just the parents, which is easy to forget, especially when you have three children to feed, clothe, and keep alive. It also reminded me how much fun we have together as a couple. And for us, it's the best therapy money can buy.

To be completely honest with you, there have been moments in the middle of our life together where I seriously wondered if we were going to make it. I remember one night a few years ago, sitting on the couch in the dark while Joe told me that this whole relationship deal wasn't working for him. He wasn't happy. "Things felt off," and he didn't want to spend the rest of his life feeling like that way. He felt neglected, like our kids were getting the best part of me.

If relationships have seasons, we were in the depths of winter with no sign of spring.

Things had been super stressful around our house. I resented that he was working so much, and we were drowning in debt thanks to heavily investing in a failed start-up. Pretty much the last thing I felt like doing was laying down next to this man who I had committed my life to, but who I felt no emotional connection with anymore.

It seems to me that our deepest desires, as well as our deepest regrets, come from the same place — our connection to others. And so often in marriage that connection has something to do with sex. It never ceases to amaze me that sex can be so dichotomous. With the same potential to create an ecstatic emotional connection as it has to be a source of profound isolation, shame or loneliness.

I cried myself to sleep that night, wrestling with having to make a decision to show up in my own life. The pressing emotions of the day had hijacked my passion. I was exhausted, and pretty much the last person I wanted to have to give more attention to was my husband. But if we were going to make it, I was going to have to regain a sense of passion. I had to realize that sex was a powerful force in my marriage.

And I don't think I am alone.

I believe that at certain points in our lives it becomes too easy to outsource passion and turn it into a spectator sport. We read *Fifty Shades of Grey* to stimulate a fake sense of passion rather than trying to cultivate those feelings in our real life. We watch movies where the hero is the guy who overcomes his fears, the teacher who risks her career on the inner city students, the man who courts the woman he loves boldly and unashamedly, risking humility for the sake of romantic gestures. They are honest with their feelings, express love openly. They are passionate.

I believe it is time for us to take responsibility for the passion in our lives. To choose to be unashamed and unabashed with our partners. To ask for what we need and to initiate sex. To become passionate about seducing our husbands.

My Saturday night date night reminded me that I want to grow old with Joe. Not because we have children together or because we signed a silly piece of paper with some official sounding words on it, but because I enjoy him. He makes me laugh and soothes my nerves when I freak out about situations I have no control over. He knows me better than anyone in the whole world and is willing to play truth or dare with me in a crowded restaurant. I was reminded that he is the one I get to be my most passionate with. Regardless of the stress in our lives, spending time with Joe, just Joe, reminds me that I willingly choose him. Again and again and again.

And it is good to remember that he and I still work. That this thing we started 15 years ago when he called me out of the blue with the cheesiest pick up line you have ever heard, has turned into something deeper and more passionate than I could have hoped. And just for the record, he still uses cheesy pick up lines on me to ensure a date night after-party. And they still work.

P.S. I know that there are a lot of situations when sexuality and passion can be sources of pain in our lives. If you are in a relationship where you don't feel safe to express your sexuality in a healthy way, or are facing painful issues like infidelity, pornography, abuse or have situations in your past that have shaped your feelings of sexuality, please talk with someone. Our secrets hold us captive. Contact me at marioto@mops.org if you need a recommendation for a professional with a trusted ear.

Questions

What were the attitudes about sex in my family as I was growing up?

What inhibits me from being free to express myself sexually?

How has my sexual relationship enabled me to know my husband physically or emotionally that otherwise would not have been possible?

Sex is a metaphor for the passion in our lives. How you do sex says a lot about how you do life. What is my sex life saying about the amount of passion I have in my life?

What is one thing I can do this week to be more passionate?

Courage to Rest

by Alexandra Kuykendall

"Rest and be thankful." — William Wordsworth

I can hear the screaming even now. The baby's. Only two hours after her last feeding, ready to eat again. And mine, in my head, screaming "NOOOOOOO" as I pull myself to consciousness and think HOW is it possibly time ALREADY?! The thought of opening my eyes makes me recoil at the sound of my own baby's cry because she is ready to wake up. AND I AM NOT.

When I think of the word rest, I think of a Grandpa on a sunny afternoon, with a choice: Do I snooze or watch TV in my recliner? And in the end it's a toggling between the two. I don't think of my attempts at mid-day naps — trying to lie down with one eye open to make sure the two year old doesn't get into the cleaning products under the sink — as "rest" because there's nothing restful about always being on.

I find the idea of rest elusive, something that I'll never grasp, that is constantly slipping out of my hands. Because really when will I ever catch up on my sleep? Feel rested? But maybe sleep and rest are connected, but not the same.

There's a difference between being totally and completely exhausted and needing space. Exhaustion requires uninterrupted sleep. Pure and simple hours with a head on a pillow and no one kicking me in the face as some sort of child-to-mommy torture. Exhaustion clouds my thinking, my emotions and my general ability to function. I've put formula in the coffee filter and sputtered pure and total nonsense as a result of lack of sleep.

Rest on the other hand is stillness. A letting down to recharge that isn't driven by my body's need to sleep, though it can recharge me, but rather my need for space — empty space — in my hours. It is quiet. It is taking a break, putting my feet up. It is a discipline that I must do to have the space to remember who I am.

In a house with four children I often can't hear myself think. The TV, the Wii, the Facebook, the screaming, the "She bit me!" and the "She's in my spot," and the cell phone and the home phone and the emails and the neighbor's dog, my mind simply doesn't have the space to stop and rest. I need a mental pause everyday, where I am not consuming or working to block out the noise, I am just sitting or lying in silence, and, well... resting. A place where I can let my thoughts wander to wherever they need to go.

A time-out is really what I need. Though my behavior often warrants a time-out — no one else is putting me in them (okay not totally true, my husband has told me to take a walk a few times). For the most part I must be the one to create space where I'm alone. I've locked myself in my bedroom, in my office, to just get a break from the whining, the bickering. These have been points where I've known I'm about to explode, or already have, and need to remove myself from the situation so I don't further rack up my children's future therapy bill. But these moments of survival are not rest. They are keeping me safe and my children safe by letting me count to ten. Alone.

No, rest must be proactive. Because really it doesn't happen on its own. I don't naturally take twenty minutes to read for fun, or listen to music while drinking cocoa on a snowy day. I try and then I notice the shoes all over the living room floor and I get up and start un-resting. No, I must be mindful that the intentional stopping and being still is not only lovely, it's required for my sanity. It is a preemptive strike against those explosions. Which is not just good for me, it's good for my entire family.

So back to the mental quiet and lack of it. As I write this I am in a month long fast from Facebook and Internet surfing. Really? You might ask. Is that necessary? And there is an unequivocal "yes" as my answer before you've even finished asking the question.

 I'd come to a breaking point. A spot where I knew my impulse was to reach for my phone or my computer or my iPad any time I had a free minute. I wasn't using those pockets of time to connect with my kids while waiting in the car or my husband after dinner, I was wasting away hours and days behind a screen.

And I certainly wasn't using those minutes to rest. To have silence of mind for a minute, to collect myself, to think about the day and what was ahead or even the next hour and create a strategy for how I was going to tackle car seats and school pick-up and four sets of hands that required mittens. I knew I needed a break, a rest.

And you know what has surprised me? Not the extra hours in the day — that's just plain embarrassing that I spend so many waking hours reading about other people's daily experiences instead of living my own. Not rediscovering a new joy in my life by removing a constant structure of comparisons and affirmation from Facebook likes — I was expecting that. What I'm finding is I have to deal with my reality. I can't push the negative feelings away by going mind-numb looking at virtual junk food. I have to deal with whatever reality is in front of me, both the spontaneous, surprising, life-filled moments and the difficult, I'd rather escape mentally moments.

It's not always comfortable (Wait! Isn't rest supposed to feel good?), but it does ground me to remember who I am and for what I was made. Despite what my actions might tell the world, I am NOT made to spend hours reading links posted on Twitter every day. I am made to love God and others with my whole self. Rest gives me the intentional space to remind me of that.

From the essay, "Super Bowl Sunday" in his book, *Prayers for a Privileged People* (Abingdon Press, 2008), Walter Brueggemann prays,

Give us some distance from the noise,
some reserve about the loud success of the day,
that we may remember that our life consists
not in things we consume,
but in neighbors we embrace.

Often I need a rest from all of the noise I consume — mental and literal — to best be able to embrace the people around me. It's often way more unnatural and uncomfortable than I think it should be, but I know it is good. For me, and for the people I love.

Questions

Do I need sleep or rest? Or both?

How do I define rest?

Does rest come naturally to me?

In what ways do I experience quiet?

What do I consume that prevents me from resting?

Courage To Be a Mom

by Mandy Arioto

"Sometimes heaven is just a new pair of glasses." — Anne Lamott

I find it fascinating that the one question our culture uses to define identity and worth is, "What do you do?" Start a conversation with someone on an airplane and without fail one of the first questions that gets asked is, "What kind of work do you show up to everyday?" And the greatest tragedy in this whole conversation is the response I heard at a party last week. A friend of ours asked a new woman he was meeting what she did for a living and this woman's cheeks blushed and she sheepishly said, "Oh, I'm just a mom." I cannot tell you the number of times I have heard these same words used by my friends and in my own head. What?

Just a mom.

It seems that what me and so many of my mom friends are missing out on is a sense of vocation. A high brow word that comes to us from ancient Latin speakers who called it "vocacio" which literally means a call or summons. It is the deep-seated knowledge that your current circumstances are part of your life's work. That what you have before you today and tomorrow are holy opportunities. That you were created with a purpose, and that your destiny is to participate with God to write a good future.

For many of us, the tension lies in the fact that we are trying to hold together a sense of identity. We are wrestling with a desire to use our education or natural talents, or to pursue a career that will help us to feel like we are our best selves. And the biggest challenge is that we are trying to do all of this while facing the very real limitations that accompany the different seasons of motherhood.

What I need to continue to remind myself of is that this mothering gig is a vocation. A calling toward holy work. That all work is God's work, and there is profound meaning in the tasks right before me. In other words, even the mundane brings him glory. All of the to-dos that accompany my vocation of motherhood matter to God.

A few weeks ago the stomach flu descended upon our house in all its fury. And for three days straight, I snuggled next to sick babies and cleaned throw-up and rubbed warm backs. And while all of these very human things were happening, a quote came to me from an author named Elizabeth Elliot, she says,

"This job has been given to me to do. Therefore it is a gift. Therefore it is a privilege. Therefore it is an offering I may make to God, therefore it is to be done gladly, if it is done for him. Here, not somewhere else, I may learn God's way. In this job and not in some other way. God looks for faithfulness."

I am convinced that finding the courage to be a mom is the bravest work to which you may ever give yourself. It is the kind of courage that chooses to show up in the best ways you know how. It is a choice to find your calling in the midst of your very real day. And it is the kind of work that will never reciprocate with material rewards or accolades.

Have you ever attended an elementary school performance? I attended a kindergarten musical extravaganza last year that was just about the most precious experience I have ever witnessed. My favorite part of the whole performance was when all of the kids walked onto the stage. My daughter Charlotte was standing in the second row on the right hand side. I watched her take her place and then she began to scan the crowd. Her eyes searched frantically until she met my gaze. Her eyes lit up and she offered me an enthusiastic wave that said, "I see you!" I am her home base. Her focal point in times of uncertainty and doubt. She is relieved. She is seen. I may not be the perfect mom, but I am the lighthouse who guides her home.

Being a mom means we are called. Called to raise generations. Called to be the brightest light that beacons our kids toward wholeness. The world is holding its breath, hanging on our every word. Waiting for us to speak into existence love and hope within our children's souls. Every act of love we offer — no matter how small — affirms worth, calms fears and teaches our chidren to do the same.

Each day (whether we are ready or not) we step up to the plate and do the best we can. As moms we learn compassion and empathy, and we become braver and more courageous — reaching deep inside our hearts to do what needs to be done. Because that's what mom's are called to do.

When you are a mom, it all matters.

Kissing that boo boo and putting band-aids on, just because. That matters.

Watching your kids do the same tricks over and over again on the trampoline and each time acting as if it was the most impressive trick you have ever seen. That matters.

Snuggling on the couch and telling stories in a silly voice. That matters.

Waking at dawn and kissing goodnight. That matters.

These holy moments matter to your kiddo, and they matter to the world.

For the rest of history, echoes of your voice will be heard.
Too often we are cruel to ourselves. We tell ourselves things that aren't true. We lay awake at night, shaming ourselves for all the things we aren't, or haven't done. Or we go through the day thinking that if somehow we just fed our kids a little bit healthier or read one more story or were a little more patient, then we would be enough.

So, just in case today is one of those days when you are wondering if what you are doing really matters ...

Wondering if anyone notices,
If anything you are doing is world-changing,
Feeling like your shoulders are heavy with worry,
If you woke up today already looking forward to bedtime —

Here is the truth for the day:

Motherhood is your worthy calling for today — and you are enough.

Questions

When was the last time someone asked you what you do for a living? What was your answer?

The tangible paycheck for your work is low. How else are you rewarded by motherhood?

What is one thing you can do today to embrace your vocation as a mom?

Courage To Be You, Bravely

by Mandy Arioto

"To be nobody but yourself in a world that's doing its best to make you somebody else, is to fight the hardest battle you are ever going to fight. Never stop fighting." — e.e. cummings

My girls are playing in the front yard as I sit on a $2 thrift-store-find knitted blanket. They are making mud pies decorated with flowers and leaves and sticks. Our neighbors joined them a few minutes ago and now they are engaged in a deep conversation about worms and caterpillars.

Each kid in my front yard is so unique. Charlotte is funny. Everyone who meets her is drawn to her laughter and ability to make any activity fun. Ellie is a leader and feels her feelings with such tremendous passion that it is both infuriating and inspiring at the same time. Neighbor Ava is sweet and gentle. She is watchful to make sure that each and every earthworm is treated with humane respect. And Ava's little sister Olivia observes the older girls to learn exactly the right technique for building mud pies. These kids manage to make sure that everyone gets what they need while laughing so loudly that the neighbors across the street keep looking out the window with disapproving frowns to try to convince me that I should reign them in. But I can't. Because I am inspired. Watching them play I would think that being yourself would be the easiest, most natural thing in the world to do.

But it isn't.

When my son Joseph was five he asked me a question, "Who are you?" I thought he was being silly so I answered, "I am your mom!" To which he replied, "No, who are you really?" I kept attempting answers but nothing seemed to really answer what he was asking. Eventually he lost interest in the conversation but I was shaken.

Who are you really?

Why is this such a hard question to answer?

At different stages of my life I would have answered that question in different ways.

In elementary school I was an over-achiever. The teacher's pet who got away with too much, because I got good grades and was nice to people.

In high school I was defined by the sports I played and the boy I was dating. My identity was determined by the words my peers spoke over me.

Then in college my free spirit took flight and I was drawn to subversive theology and the ruffling of feathers.

And now, at the age of 36, I am realizing that in spite of all the personas I tried on, I lost myself along the way.

So much of who we grow up to be is less DNA and more habit. From a very young age we are conditioned to act in certain ways in order to feel loved and accepted. Expectations are placed on us, and we begin to think that they are universal truths rather than the individual expectations of one person or family or school or church or group of friends. This is the beginning of our loss of authenticity.

It's very difficult after you have banked twenty years and fifty thousand dollars in student loans to become someone else, to regain your sense of self. It takes no small effort to relearn who you were created to be.

What has been written into your soul since the beginning of time?

All of us are pilgrims on a common quest. Searching for mecca, a holy land that we will recognize only after we arrive. A place where we will know what we have been placed on this earth to do and be. We spend our lifetime searching for answers, wandering toward the unique space we were placed on this earth to fill, because being human is more than water and dust.

I believe that being human is a gift. A sometimes awkward gift that makes you intensely happy and intensely needy at the same time.

Our humanity — this process of becoming yourself — takes bravery. It means saying your truest feelings, confronting your fears about what other people will think of you and figuring out what you really like. And most of the time it isn't created by big life altering actions. Instead, the process of becoming yourself is a series of small, sometimes trivial choices that when bound together create the most wholly-beautiful version of you.

Do you ever feel like you are surrounded by a culture that wants to standardize you? Telling you to wear the same clothes, to think the same thoughts and buy the same products? I can even see it in so many of our faith communities who unintentionally steer us toward conformity. But something in my gut tells me this is wrong. Because our creator is an artist — and every artist friend I have will tell you that they have no interest in creating replicate-able art.

The good news for all of us who strive to maintain our spark — who resist standardization by clawing our way toward becoming ourselves — is that all the time we spend pressing against conformity is time spent fighting to recognize God's artistry in ourselves, and to let that artistry make us whole.

How do we embark on the journey of becoming more ourselves?

Confront your broken places. The process of mending starts with identifying the torn places. Sometimes this process is painful. It starts with assessing the ways that our souls have been chipped by the words of others, or by our own shame. A lifelong friend of mine who has been saved by AA once told me that healing begins when we wake up and say, "Enough!" Being the truest version of ourselves first requires *admitting* our brokenness. It might feel like a huge act of disloyalty to the boundaries that you have built to make sense of your life. Or it might be the most freeing gift of compassion you could ever give yourself.

Figure out what you like: I have a friend who for the life of her cannot pick a pastry. We will go out for coffee and she has no idea what she really likes. She second guesses *every decision she makes* — even when it comes to deciding between a muffin and a croissant. Take some time to figure out what your real preferences are without surveying your family or friends for their opinion. Not what *should* you like, but what *do* you like.

Let go of expectations: Are you chasing someone else's version of success? Have you imposed expectations on your life that someone else gave to you? The good news is that you get to change your mind! Assess the expectations that shape your choices and throw out the ones that are holding you captive. Authentic goals are a wonderful thing, but artificial ideals set by ___ (the world, your parents, your friends, Mrs. Jones next door) can sometimes masquerade as the real thing. Take solid look at what you put your energy toward and what you call a win. Does it come from your heart, or someone else's judgment?

Try all sorts of new things: Our body is born once, but the birth of our hearts is a continual process. Every experience has the potential to bring life to new territories of your heart. Try some things you have never tried before and let those experiences help you remember who you are, and learn who you could be.

Eliminate stuff: Clean house, *literally*. Getting rid of stuff frees up room to invite new things in. This is true in our thought life and also in our "stuff" life. So give some stuff away! In so doing you will make room for a fresh start.

Reclaim your passion: Life is *painful* when you're not living out your passions. So many people feel resentful or drained because they are not expressing the gifts that are lying dormant in their hearts. If you have shelved your natural giftings, open the cupboard wide and set them free! Sing, dance, write, create — and share. You'll feel more yourself when you *share* your gifts with the world.

Be loved: We begin to be ourselves when we notice how we are already seen and loved. Do you feel pursued? Do you know the love of a God who chases you — *pursues* you with a love so consuming that he gives his very self on your behalf? When we recognize that we are loved entirely we are free to love ourselves with that same compassionate abandon.

I love seeing kids in the grocery store whose parents were brave enough to let them wear a costume that was important to them that particular day. After all, isn't childhood supposed to be the most magical time in our life? When we can believe that anything is possible? When we can construct an entire bakery out of mud and flowers? When our inner selves can be at play in the front yard — on full display — and that's okay. The possibilities of childhood are unguarded, untamed and unjaded. If only our adult decisions could be made from such a place. I am convinced that many more of us would be living a life more true to who we feel we are in our souls.

Could it be that something raw and life-giving is offering springtime to your soul?

This is your time to come alive. To be brave. To be *you*.

So, may your soul be *disturbed* when you have settled for something safe.

May you have an encounter with the God who can show you the gifts and truths that he has woven into your soul.

 And may you experience the fullness of life that comes as you decide to Be you, Bravely.

Questions

In what ways have I become a product of those around me instead of my true self?

Looking back throughout my life what personas have I tried on?

What brokenness do I need to confront in order to experience life authentically?

If I found the courage to be me, how would I change?

Authors

Alexandra Kuykendall, Sherry Surratt, Mandy Arioto

Mandy Arioto

Mandy has three kids, one dog and married her husband in spite of the fact that he used the cheesiest pickup line ever to ask her out. She and her husband recently moved from Southern California to Denver so that their kids could learn how to make snow angels and because they believe in adventures. Before joining MOPS as their Director of Marketing and Membership, Mandy was a preaching pastor at MOSAIC in San Diego. She is widely accepted as a relationship expert, and has been featured on MSN, theknot.com, thenest.com and Fox. Mandy speaks to national and international audiences on the topics of Mothering, Leadership Development and Cultural Trends. She and her husband are in the throes of raising three young kids to be adventurous, tender-hearted world changers. Share in her adventures at mandyarioto.com or at mops.org/blog.

Alexandra Kuykendall

As a mom to four girls, ages 11, 8, 4 and 2, Alexandra Kuykendall is offered daily doses of the ludicrous and sublime. She is the author of this year's MOPS International theme book, *The Artist's Daughter, A Memoir* and is the Mom and Leader Content Editor for the MOPS organization. This means she reads a lot and writes when she can. But don't be fooled by long and fancy titles, most of Alex's days are spent washing dishes, driving to and from different schools and trying to find a better solution to the laundry dilemma. You can connect with her at alexandrakuykendall.com or mops.org/blog

Sherry Surratt

Sherry Surratt is the visionary CEO and President of MOPS International. Before coming to MOPS, she served as the Director for Innovation Labs at Leadership Network, a church leadership organization based in Dallas. She joined Leadership Network in 2008 with an extensive background in ministry, formally serving as Central Support Pastor for Seacoast Church in Mt. Pleasant, SC. Sherry also has a background in education and was a teacher and administrator in the Houston public school system. She and her pastor husband, Geoff Surratt, reside in Colorado, and are parents of two adult children, Mike and Brittainy, and the proud grandparents of Maggie Claire and Mollie Rose. Her new book, *Just Lead!,* is getting rave reviews for its insightful wisdom for women leaders. Be on the lookout for Sherry's upcoming book *Brave Mom: Facing and Overcoming Your Real Mom Fears* comes out October 2014 and takes an honest look at what moms really fear and what you can do about it. Find her at sherrysurratt.com.

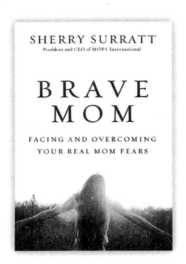

SHERRY SURRATT
President and CEO of MOPS International

BRAVE
MOM

FACING AND OVERCOMING
YOUR REAL MOM FEARS

Brave Mom: Facing and Overcoming Your Real Mom Fears

Releasing in October of 2014, this new book by MOPS CEO Sherry Surratt is a mom manifesto. Sherry looks at all of the reasonable and unreasonable fears that we have as moms and offers real-life stories and insights into how to face them with courage. Inspiring and warm-hearted, this book will encourage you to be a brave mom.

Mothers of Preschoolers

MOPS International, Inc. // 2370 South Trenton Way // Denver CO 80231-3822 // 303.733.5353 // MOPS.org